2222 Short One-Liner & Funny Jokes Copy

The Punny Joke Book to Keep Kids, Children, and Everyone Full of Laughing Medicine

Penny Punsworth

Copyright © 2024 Penny Punsworth

All rights reserved. No part of this publication may be reproduced, distributed or transmitted in any form or by any means, including photocopying, recording, or other electronic or mechanical methods, without the prior written permission of the publisher, except in the case of brief quotations embodied in critical reviews and certain other non-commercial uses permitted by copyright law.

Trademarked names appear throughout this book. Rather than use a trademark symbol with every occurrence of a trademarked name, names are used in an editorial fashion, with no intention of infringement of the respective owner's trademark. The information in this book is distributed on an "as is" basis, without warranty. Although every precaution has been taken in the preparation of this work, neither the author nor the publisher shall have any liability to any person or entity with respect to any loss or damage caused or alleged to be caused directly or indirectly by the information contained in this book.

Contents

1. Alien Jokes   1
2. Animal Jokes   3
3. Anniversary Jokes   6
4. Art Jokes   8
5. Award Jokes   10
6. Baker Jokes   13
7. Barista Jokes   15
8. Bartender Jokes   17
9. Beer Jokes   19
10. Book Jokes   21
11. Camping Jokes   23
12. Car Jokes   25
13. Carnival Jokes   27
14. Celebration Jokes   29
15. Chef Jokes   31
16. Circus Jokes   33

17.	Classic Jokes	35
18.	Clown Jokes	36
19.	Coffee Jokes	38
20.	Comedian Jokes	40
21.	Competition Jokes	42
22.	Computer Jokes	44
23.	Contemporary Jokes	45
24.	Crime Jokes	46
25.	Dad Jokes	48
26.	Dance Jokes	49
27.	Dinosaur Jokes	51
28.	Doctor Jokes	53
29.	Fairy Tale Jokes	56
30.	Fantasy Jokes	58
31.	Fashion Jokes	60
32.	Festival Jokes	62
33.	Fishing Jokes	64
34.	Fitness Jokes	66
35.	Food Jokes	68
36.	Friendship Jokes	70
37.	Game Show Jokes	72
38.	Gaming Jokes	74

39.	Gardening Jokes	76
40.	Geography Jokes	78
41.	Ghost Jokes	80
42.	Graduation Jokes	82
43.	Health Jokes	84
44.	Hiking Jokes	86
45.	Historical Jokes	88
46.	Holiday Jokes	90
47.	Holiday Season Jokes	92
48.	Impressionist Jokes	94
49.	Internet Jokes	96
50.	Kids Jokes	98
51.	Knock-Knock Jokes	99
52.	Lawyer Jokes	104
53.	Library Jokes	107
54.	Light Bulb Jokes	109
55.	Magician Jokes	112
56.	Marriage Jokes	114
57.	Math Jokes	116
58.	Medical Jokes	118
59.	Movie Jokes	120
60.	Music Jokes	122

61.	Mystery Jokes	124
62.	Nature Jokes	126
63.	Office Jokes	128
64.	Parenting Jokes	130
65.	Pet Jokes	132
66.	Photography Jokes	134
67.	Pirate Jokes	136
68.	Plane Jokes	138
69.	Podcast Jokes	140
70.	Political Jokes	142
71.	Random Jokes	144
72.	Reality TV Jokes	145
73.	Relationship Jokes	147
74.	Retirement Jokes	148
75.	Road Trip Jokes	150
76.	School Jokes	152
77.	Sci-Fi Jokes	156
78.	Science Jokes	158
79.	Senior Jokes	160
80.	Shopping Jokes	163
81.	Short Jokes	165
82.	Sibling Jokes	166

83.	Social Media Jokes	168
84.	Space Jokes	170
85.	Sports Jokes	172
86.	Student Jokes	174
87.	Superhero Jokes	176
88.	TV Jokes	178
89.	Talent Show Jokes	180
90.	Teacher Jokes	182
91.	Tech Jokes	184
92.	Technology Jokes	186
93.	Theater Jokes	188
94.	Train Jokes	190
95.	Travel Jokes	192
96.	Vacation Jokes	194
97.	Vegetarian Jokes	196
98.	Waiter Jokes	198
99.	Weather Jokes	200
100.	Wine Jokes	202
101.	Work Jokes	204
102.	Zookeeper Jokes	206

Alien Jokes

Why don't aliens ever get lost? Because they always follow the UFO.

How do you organize an alien invasion? You plan-et.

Why did the alien go to school? To improve its space knowledge.

Why don't some aliens ever get tired? Because they're always out of this world.

What do you call an alien that tells jokes? A pun-iverse.

Why was the alien always calm? It knew how to stay grounded.

What's an alien's favorite type of music? Space jam.

Why did the alien bring a ladder to the spaceship? To reach new heights.

How do you make an alien laugh? Tell it a space-tacular joke.

Why did the alien stay at the spa? To get a little extra relaxation.

What do you call a lazy alien? A space-sloth.

Why don't some aliens play sports? They're afraid of the competition.

How do you keep an alien from getting lost? Use a space map.

What's an alien's favorite game? Space tag.

Why did the alien go to therapy? It had too many issues.

What's an alien's favorite book? The Hitchhiker's Guide to the Galaxy.

Why was the alien so confident? It knew it was always on solid ground.

How do you make an alien dance? Put a little boogie in it.

Why did the alien bring a map to the adventure? To find its way.

What do you call an alien with no patience? A slow-etic.

Why did the alien go to the doctor? It wasn't feeling too well.

What's an alien's favorite movie? E.T. the Extra-Terrestrial.

Why did the alien go on a diet? To stay healthy.

What do you call an alien who loves to sing? A space-melody.

How do you organize an alien race? You set the space-craft.

Animal Jokes

Why don't seagulls fly over the bay? Because then they'd be bagels!

Why do cows wear bells? Because their horns don't work.

Why don't oysters share their pearls? Because they're shellfish.

What do you call a fish with no eyes? Fsh.

Why did the duck get a detention? For fowl language.

How do you catch a squirrel? Climb up in a tree and act like a nut!

What do you call a cow with no legs? Ground beef.

Why did the elephant bring a suitcase to the zoo? He wanted to pack his trunk!

Why do fish always know how much they weigh? Because they have their own scales.

What do you call an alligator in a vest? An investigator.

What do you call a lazy kangaroo? A pouch potato.

Why did the frog take the bus to work today? His car got toad.

Why are frogs so happy? Because they eat whatever bugs them!

What do you call a bear with no teeth? A gummy bear.

Why was the cat sitting on the computer? To keep an eye on the mouse!

What do you call a sleeping bull? A bulldozer.

Why don't cows wear shoes? Because they lactose.

How do you count cows? With a cowculator.

What do you get from a pampered cow? Spoiled milk.

Why did the sheep go to the beach? To get a little baa-lance.

What do you call a fly without wings? A walk.

Why was the big cat disqualified from the race? Because it was a cheetah.

What do you get when you cross a snowman and a dog? Frostbite.

How do cows stay up to date? They read the moos-paper.

Why did the scarecrow become a successful animal trainer? He was outstanding in his field.

What's a cat's favorite color? Purr-ple.

Why don't some fish play the piano? Because you can't tuna fish.

Why did the dog sit in the shade? It didn't want to be a hot dog.

Why don't oysters donate to charity? Because they're shellfish.

What do you call a snowman with a six-pack? An abdominal snowman.

Why did the cow become an astronaut? To see the moooon.

Why did the chicken join a band? Because it had the drumsticks.

Why don't some animals use computers? They're afraid of the mouse.

What's a cat's favorite movie? The Sound of Mewsic.

How do sheep greet each other at Christmas? Merry Christmas to ewe!

What's a cow's favorite holiday? Moo Year's Eve.

How do bees get to school? By school buzz.

Why did the lion eat the tightrope walker? It wanted a well-balanced meal.

What's a dog's favorite city? New Yorkie.

Why did the monkey like the banana? Because it had appeal.

Why don't some animals play cards? Because there are too many cheetahs.

Anniversary Jokes

Why did the scarecrow become an anniversary planner? He was outstanding in his field.

Why don't some couples get lost on their anniversary? They always follow the love map.

How do you organize an anniversary celebration? You plan-et.

Why don't some anniversaries ever get boring? They always have love.

What do you call an anniversary planner that tells jokes? A pun-iversary planner.

Why was the couple always calm? They knew how to stay in love.

Why did the couple bring a ladder to the celebration? To reach new heights.

How do you make an anniversary couple laugh? Tell them a love joke.

What do you call a lazy anniversary planner? A slack-celebrator.

Why don't some anniversaries ever get boring? They always have fun.

How do you keep a couple from getting lost? Use a love map.

What's a couple's favorite game? The Newlywed Game.

Why did the couple go to therapy? They had too many unresolved issues.

What's a couple's favorite book? The Notebook.

Why was the anniversary couple so confident? They knew they were always the main event.

How do you make an anniversary couple dance? Put a little boogie in it.

Why did the couple bring a map to the celebration? To find their way.

What do you call a couple with no patience? A slow partner.

Why did the couple go to the doctor? They weren't feeling too romantic.

What's a couple's favorite movie? Love Actually.

Why did the couple go on a diet? To stay fit for the celebration.

What do you call a couple who loves to sing? A love duet.

Art Jokes

Why don't artists ever get lost? They always follow their muse.

How do you organize an art show? You plan-et.

Why did the painter go to school? To improve his brush strokes.

Why don't some artists ever get tired? They're always inspired.

What do you call an artist that tells jokes? A pun-casso.

Why was the sculptor always calm? He knew how to stay grounded.

What's an artist's favorite type of music? Classical.

Why did the painter bring a ladder to the studio? To reach new heights.

How do you make an artist laugh? Tell them a colorful joke.

Why did the artist stay at the spa? To get a little extra relaxation.

What do you call a lazy artist? A slack-canvas.

Why don't some artists play sports? They're afraid of missing the mark.

How do you keep an artist from getting lost? Use a gallery map.

What's an artist's favorite game? Pictionary.

Why did the artist go to therapy? He had too many unresolved issues.

What's an artist's favorite book? The Picture of Dorian Gray.

Why was the artist so confident? He knew he was always on solid ground.

How do you make an artist dance? Put a little boogie in it.

Why did the artist bring a map to the gallery? To find his way.

What do you call an artist with no patience? A slow-brush.

Why did the artist go to the doctor? He wasn't feeling too well.

What's an artist's favorite movie? The Art of Getting By.

Why did the artist go on a diet? To stay fit for the easel.

What do you call an artist who loves to sing? A brush-with-melody.

How do you make a painter cry? Draw their tears.

Award Jokes

1. Why don't award recipients get lost? They always follow the recognition.

2. How do you organize an award ceremony? You plan-et.

3. Why did the actor go to school? To improve his acceptance speech.

4. Why don't award shows ever get boring? They always have stars.

5. What do you call an award that tells jokes? A pun-ny trophy.

6. Why was the award winner always calm? They knew how to stay grounded.

7. What's an award recipient's favorite type of music? Winning anthems.

8. Why did the award winner bring a ladder to the stage? To reach new heights.

9. How do you make an award winner laugh? Tell them a prestigious joke.

10. Why did the nominee stay at the spa? To get a little extra relaxation.

11. What do you call a lazy award recipient? A slack-olade.

12. Why don't some awards ever get tired? They always stay polished.

13. How do you keep an award from getting lost? Use a trophy map.

14. What's an award winner's favorite game? Prize pursuit.

15. Why did the award winner go to therapy? They had too many unresolved issues.

16. What's an award recipient's favorite book? The Prize.

17. Why was the award winner so confident? They knew they were always the best.

18. How do you make an award winner dance? Put a little boogie in it.

19. Why did the winner bring a map to the ceremony? To find their way.

20. What do you call an award recipient with no patience? A slow laureate.

21. Why did the nominee go to the doctor? They weren't feeling too celebratory.

22. What's an award winner's favorite movie? The Artist.

23. Why did the award recipient go on a diet? To stay fit for the spotlight.

24. What do you call an award winner who loves to sing? A golden crooner.

25.

Baker Jokes

Why did the scarecrow become a baker? He was outstanding in his field.

Why don't some bakers get lost? They always follow the recipe.

How do you organize a bake sale? You plan-et.

Why don't some bakers ever get tired? They always rise to the occasion.

What do you call a baker that tells jokes? A pun-derful baker.

Why was the baker always calm? He knew how to stay cool under pressure.

What's a baker's favorite type of music? Rock 'n' roll (with a little butter).

Why did the baker bring a ladder to the bakery? To reach the top shelf.

How do you make a baker laugh? Tell them a well-kneaded joke.

Why did the baker stay at the spa? To get a little extra relaxation.

What do you call a lazy baker? A slack-dough.

Why don't some bakers play sports? They're afraid of getting in a jam.

How do you keep a baker from getting lost? Use a recipe map.

What's a baker's favorite game? Cooking Mama.

Why did the baker go to therapy? He had too many issues to knead out.

What's a baker's favorite book? Like Water for Chocolate.

Why was the baker so confident? He knew he was always on top of things.

How do you make a baker dance? Put a little boogie in it.

Why did the baker bring a map to the market? To find the freshest ingredients.

What do you call a baker with no patience? A slow riser.

Why did the baker go to the doctor? He wasn't feeling too well-done.

What's a baker's favorite movie? Ratatouille.

Why did the baker go on a diet? To stay fit for the bakery.

What do you call a baker who loves to sing? A crooner.

Barista Jokes

Why did the scarecrow become a barista? He was outstanding in his field.

Why don't some baristas get lost? They always follow the coffee recipe.

How do you organize a coffee shop? You plan-et.

Why don't some baristas ever get tired? They always have a shot of energy.

What do you call a barista that tells jokes? A pun-derful brewer.

Why was the barista always calm? He knew how to stay grounded.

What's a barista's favorite type of music? Smooth jazz.

Why did the barista bring a ladder to the coffee shop? To reach the top shelf.

How do you make a barista laugh? Tell them a latte joke.

Why did the barista stay at the spa? To get a little extra relaxation.

What do you call a lazy barista? A slack-tender.

Why don't some baristas play sports? They're afraid of getting in a pickle.

How do you keep a barista from getting lost? Use a coffee map.

What's a barista's favorite game? Pour-it.

Why did the barista go to therapy? He had too many mixed emotions.

What's a barista's favorite book? The Joy of Coffee.

Why was the barista so confident? He knew he was always on top of things.

How do you make a barista dance? Put a little boogie in it.

Why did the barista bring a map to the market? To find the freshest beans.

What do you call a barista with no patience? A slow pourer.

Why did the barista go to the doctor? He wasn't feeling too well-mixed.

What's a barista's favorite movie? Coffee and Cigarettes.

Why did the barista go on a diet? To stay fit for the coffee shop.

What do you call a barista who loves to sing? A crooner.

Bartender Jokes

Why don't some bartenders get lost? They always follow the recipe.

How do you organize a bar night? You plan-et.

Why don't some bartenders ever get tired? They always have a shot of energy.

What do you call a bartender that tells jokes? A pun-derful mixer.

Why was the bartender always calm? He knew how to stay cool under pressure.

What's a bartender's favorite type of music? Smooth jazz.

Why did the bartender bring a ladder to the bar? To reach the top shelf.

How do you make a bartender laugh? Tell them a spirited joke.

Why did the bartender stay at the spa? To get a little extra relaxation.

What do you call a lazy bartender? A slack-tender.

Why don't some bartenders play sports? They're afraid of getting in a pickle.

How do you keep a bartender from getting lost? Use a recipe map.

What's a bartender's favorite game? Pour-it.

Why did the bartender go to therapy? He had too many mixed emotions.

What's a bartender's favorite book? The Joy of Mixology.

Why was the bartender so confident? He knew he was always on top of things.

How do you make a bartender dance? Put a little boogie in it.

Why did the bartender bring a map to the market? To find the freshest ingredients.

What do you call a bartender with no patience? A slow pourer.

Why did the bartender go to the doctor? He wasn't feeling too well-mixed.

What's a bartender's favorite movie? Cocktail.

Why did the bartender go on a diet? To stay fit for the bar.

What do you call a bartender who loves to sing? A crooner.

Beer Jokes

Why don't beers ever get lost? Because they always know their way back to the bar.

What's a skeleton's least favorite room? The living room.

Why did the scarecrow become a bartender? He was outstanding in his field.

How do you organize a beer party? You plan-et.

Why did the beer go to school? To get a little more fizz-education.

Why did the beer break up with the wine? It needed some space.

What's a beer's favorite type of music? Brewgrass.

Why did the beer go to therapy? It had too many issues.

Why don't beers tell jokes? Because they might get too foamy.

How do you stop a beer from talking? Put a cap on it.

Why was the beer so good at baseball? It knew how to pitch.

What's a beer's favorite game? Hopscotch.

Why did the beer bring a ladder to the bar? To reach new heights.

Why did the beer go to the gym? To get a little more hops.

What do you call a beer that tells jokes? A brew-haha.

Why did the beer get promoted? It was a great draft pick.

What's a beer's favorite movie? Brew's Brothers.

How do beers greet each other? "Cheers!"

Why did the beer stay at the spa? To get a little extra hop therapy.

Why was the beer always invited to parties? Because it brought a lot of bubbly personality.

Why did the beer file a police report? It got mugged.

How do you make a beer dance? Put a little hop in it.

Why was the beer so confident? It knew it was always a good pour.

What's a beer's favorite book? Brewster's Millions.

Why did the beer go to the doctor? It was feeling a little flat.

Book Jokes

Why did the book join the police? It wanted to go undercover.

Why don't books play hide and seek? Because they're always getting read.

How do you organize a space-themed library? You planet.

Why did the librarian get kicked off the plane? Because it was overbooked.

What's a book's favorite type of music? Covers.

Why did the book cross the road? To find its plot.

Why don't books make good comedians? They're always getting shelved.

What do you call a book about electricity? A current novel.

Why was the science book so smart? Because it had all the answers.

Why don't libraries have lights? Because books are always bright enough.

Why was the history book always tired? It had too many dates.

What did the book say to the librarian? "I'm checked out!"

Why do books make great friends? They're always there for you, no matter the chapter.

What's a bookworm's favorite part of the computer? The bookmarks.

Why did the detective book go to the library? To check out the mystery section.

Why don't books ever get cold? Because they have so many covers.

What do you call a book club stuck on the same book? A binding contract.

Why did the romance novel go to therapy? It had too many issues.

Why did the thriller book go to school? To improve its suspense.

What's a book's favorite holiday? Book Lovers Day.

Why don't books play sports? They're too busy being read.

What did the librarian say to the book? "You're overdue!"

Why was the cookbook always confident? It had all the right ingredients.

Why did the fantasy book go on a diet? To get its plot in shape.

Camping Jokes

Why don't some tents ever get lost? Because they always pitch in the right place.

How do you organize a camping trip? You plan-et.

Why did the scarecrow become a camper? He was outstanding in his field.

Why don't some campfires ever get lonely? Because they always have a lot of marsh-mellows.

What's a camper's favorite type of music? Rock and roll.

Why did the camper bring a ladder to the campsite? To reach the high points.

Why did the camper bring string to the campsite? To tie up loose ends.

Why don't some tents tell secrets? Because they might get pitched.

Why did the camper go to therapy? To get over his camping issues.

What did one campfire say to the other? "You light up my life."

Why don't some people ever get bored camping? Because they're always in-tents.

What's a camper's favorite game? Capture the flag.

Why did the bear break up with the camper? It found him too intense.

What do you call a lazy camper? A sloth.

Why did the camper go to the beach? To catch some rays.

What do you call a campfire that's always on time? A punctual flame.

Why don't some campers ever get lost? Because they always follow the trail.

What's a camper's favorite dessert? S'mores.

Why did the camper stay at the spa? To get a little extra relaxation.

Why was the tent always calm? Because it knew how to chill.

How do you make a campfire laugh? Tell it a s'more joke.

Why did the camper bring a map to the campsite? To find his way.

What's a camper's favorite book? Where the Wild Things Are.

Why did the camper go to the doctor? He was feeling a little campy.

Car Jokes

Why did the scarecrow become a great driver? He was outstanding in his field.

What kind of car does a Jedi drive? A Toy-Yoda.

Why don't cars play hide and seek? They always get found.

How do you organize a car show? You plan-et.

Why did the car go to school? To improve its engine-uity.

Why don't some cars ever get tired? Because they always have drive.

What do you call a car that tells jokes? A pun-derful.

Why was the car always calm? It knew how to stay in neutral.

What's a car's favorite type of music? Heavy metal.

Why did the car bring a ladder to the race? To reach the high speeds.

How do you make a car laugh? Tell it a wheel-y good joke.

Why did the car stay at the spa? To get a little extra polish.

What do you call a lazy car? A slack-liner.

Why don't some cars play sports? They're afraid of the crash.

How do you keep a car from getting lost? Use a GPS.

What's a car's favorite game? Road-trippers.

Why did the car go to therapy? It had too many issues.

What's a car's favorite book? The Great Gas-by.

Why was the car so confident? It knew it was always in the driver's seat.

How do you make a car dance? Put a little boogie in it.

Why did the car bring a map to the race? To find its way.

What do you call a car with no wheels? A runner-up.

Why did the car go to the doctor? It wasn't feeling too well.

What's a car's favorite movie? Fast and Furious.

Carnival Jokes

Why did the scarecrow join the carnival? He was outstanding in his field.

Why don't some carnival workers get lost? They always follow the midway.

How do you organize a carnival? You plan-et.

Why don't some carnival rides ever get tired? They always have ups and downs.

What do you call a carnival worker that tells jokes? A pun-slinger.

Why was the carnival barker always calm? He knew how to draw a crowd.

What's a carnival's favorite type of music? Carousel tunes.

Why did the acrobat bring a ladder to the carnival? To reach new heights.

How do you make a carnival worker laugh? Tell them a midway joke.

Why did the carousel horse stay at the spa? To get a little extra relaxation.

What do you call a lazy carnival worker? A slack-barker.

Why don't some carnival games ever get boring? They always have prizes.

How do you keep a carnival worker from getting lost? Use a midway map.

What's a carnival worker's favorite game? Ring toss.

Why did the fortune teller go to therapy? She had too many unresolved futures.

What's a carnival worker's favorite book? Something Wicked This Way Comes.

Why was the carnival performer so confident? He knew he was always on top of the show.

How do you make a carnival worker dance? Put a little boogie in it.

Why did the carnival worker bring a map to the fair? To find their way.

What do you call a carnival worker with no patience? A slow barker.

Why did the juggler go to the doctor? He wasn't feeling too balanced.

What's a carnival worker's favorite movie? Big.

Why did the strongman go on a diet? To stay fit for the feats of strength.

What do you call a carnival worker who loves to sing? A tune-spinner.

Celebration Jokes

Why did the scarecrow join the celebration? He was outstanding in his field.

Why don't some party planners get lost? They always follow the celebration.

How do you organize a celebration? You plan-et.

Why don't some celebrations ever get tired? They always have party energy.

What do you call a celebration organizer that tells jokes? A pun-derful planner.

Why was the host always calm? They knew how to stay festive.

What's a celebration's favorite type of music? Party anthems.

Why did the guest bring a ladder to the party? To reach new heights.

How do you make a celebration guest laugh? Tell them a party joke.

Why did the party-goer stay at the spa? To get a little extra relaxation.

What do you call a lazy party planner? A slack-celebrator.

Why don't some parties ever get boring? They always have fun.

How do you keep a celebration guest from getting lost? Use a party map.

What's a party host's favorite game? Pin the tail on the donkey.

Why did the party-goer go to therapy? They had too many unresolved issues.

What's a party host's favorite book? The Great Gatsby.

Why was the celebration so confident? It knew it was always the main event.

How do you make a party-goer dance? Put a little boogie in it.

Why did the host bring a map to the event? To find their way.

What do you call a party guest with no patience? A slow reveler.

Why did the guest go to the doctor? They weren't feeling too celebratory.

What's a party host's favorite movie? Project X.

Why did the party-goer go on a diet? To stay fit for the festivities.

What do you call a party guest who loves to sing? A karaoke star.

Chef Jokes

Why did the scarecrow become a chef? He was outstanding in his field.

Why don't some chefs get lost? They always follow the recipe.

How do you organize a chef's kitchen? You plan-et.

Why don't some chefs ever get tired? They always have too much on their plate.

What do you call a chef that tells jokes? A pun-derful cook.

Why was the chef always calm? He knew how to stay saucy.

What's a chef's favorite type of music? Heavy metal (for those pots and pans).

Why did the chef bring a ladder to the kitchen? To reach the top shelf.

How do you make a chef laugh? Tell them a well-seasoned joke.

Why did the chef stay at the spa? To get a little extra relaxation.

What do you call a lazy chef? A slack-sauté.

Why don't some chefs play sports? They're afraid of getting in a pickle.

How do you keep a chef from getting lost? Use a recipe map.

What's a chef's favorite game? Cooking Mama.

Why did the chef go to therapy? He had too many issues to stew over.

What's a chef's favorite book? Like Water for Chocolate.

Why was the chef so confident? He knew he was always on top of things.

How do you make a chef dance? Put a little boogie in it.

Why did the chef bring a map to the market? To find the freshest ingredients.

What do you call a chef with no patience? A slow cooker.

Why did the chef go to the doctor? He wasn't feeling too well-done.

What's a chef's favorite movie? Ratatouille.

Why did the chef go on a diet? To stay fit for the kitchen.

What do you call a chef who loves to sing? A crooner.

Circus Jokes

Why did the scarecrow join the circus? He was outstanding in his field.

Why don't some circus performers get lost? They always follow the big top.

How do you organize a circus show? You plan-et.

Why don't some circus performers ever get tired? They always have the energy for the act.

What do you call a circus performer that tells jokes? A pun-derful act.

Why was the ringmaster always calm? He knew how to stay in control.

What's a circus performer's favorite type of music? Carnival tunes.

Why did the acrobat bring a ladder to the circus? To reach new heights.

How do you make a circus performer laugh? Tell them a big top joke.

Why did the trapeze artist stay at the spa? To get a little extra relaxation.

What do you call a lazy circus performer? A slack-walker.

Why don't some circus performers play sports? They're afraid of dropping the ball.

How do you keep a circus performer from getting lost? Use a circus map.

What's a circus performer's favorite game? High-wire tag.

Why did the lion tamer go to therapy? He had too many unresolved issues.

What's a circus performer's favorite book? Water for Elephants.

Why was the circus performer so confident? He knew he was always on top of his game.

How do you make a circus performer dance? Put a little boogie in it.

Why did the juggler bring a map to the circus? To find his way.

What do you call a circus performer with no patience? A slow juggler.

Why did the clown go to the doctor? He wasn't feeling too funny.

What's a circus performer's favorite movie? The Greatest Showman.

Why did the tightrope walker go on a diet? To stay light on their feet.

What do you call a circus performer who loves to sing? A ring-melody.

Classic Jokes

I told my wife she was drawing her eyebrows too high. She looked surprised.

Why don't skeletons fight each other? They don't have the guts.

Parallel lines have so much in common. It's a shame they'll never meet.

I told my computer I needed a break, and now it won't stop sending me Kit-Kats.

Why did the bicycle fall over? Because it was two-tired!

Clown Jokes

Why did the scarecrow become a clown? He was outstanding in his field.

Why don't some clowns get lost? They always follow the laughter.

How do you organize a clown show? You plan-et.

Why don't some clowns ever get tired? They always have a laugh.

What do you call a clown that tells jokes? A pun-ny clown.

Why was the clown always calm? He knew how to stay humorous.

What's a clown's favorite type of music? Funny tunes.

Why did the clown bring a ladder to the circus? To reach new heights.

How do you make a clown laugh? Tell them a clowning-around joke.

Why did the clown stay at the spa? To get a little extra relaxation.

What do you call a lazy clown? A slack-nose.

Why don't some clowns play sports? They're afraid of dropping the ball.

How do you keep a clown from getting lost? Use a circus map.

What's a clown's favorite game? Clown tag.

Why did the clown go to therapy? He had too many unresolved issues.

What's a clown's favorite book? The Clown in the Gown Drives the Car with the Star.

Why was the clown so confident? He knew he was always on top of his game.

How do you make a clown dance? Put a little boogie in it.

Why did the clown bring a map to the circus? To find his way.

What do you call a clown with no patience? A slow jester.

What's a clown's favorite movie? It.

Why did the clown go on a diet? To stay in shape for the performance.

What do you call a clown who loves to sing? A honk-melody.

Coffee Jokes

How does a coffee bean feel after a good workout? Strong and brewed.

Why did the coffee taste like mud? Because it was ground just a few minutes ago.

Why did the espresso keep checking his watch? Because he was pressed for time.

How do coffee beans say goodbye? They wave.

What did the coffee say to the sugar? You make life sweet.

Why don't snakes drink coffee? Because it makes them viperactive.

Why did the coffee go to the police station? It got mugged.

What's a coffee's favorite spell? Espresso Patronum.

Why did the coffee bean keep checking his watch? Because he was running out of time.

How does Moses make his coffee? Hebrews it.

Why was the coffee so confident? It knew it was a brew-tiful day.

What did the coffee say to the sugar cube? You complete me.

Why don't coffee beans ever gossip? They don't spill the beans.

What do you call a sad cup of coffee? A depresso.

Why do coffee beans never get lost? They know the grind.

How does a tech guy drink coffee? He installs Java.

Why did the coffee go to therapy? It had too much latte on its mind.

What did the coffee say when it was feeling down? I'm brewing up trouble.

Why was the coffee so popular at parties? Because it was always perking up the conversation.

Why do coffee beans always tell the truth? Because they never tell tall tales.

How did the hipster burn his tongue? He drank his coffee before it was cool.

Why did the coffee file for divorce? Because it was grounded.

Why are coffee beans such good friends? Because they're always brewing up fun.

What's a coffee's favorite karaoke song? Hit Me With Your Best Shot.

Comedian Jokes

Why did the scarecrow become a comedian? He was outstanding in his field.

Why don't some comedians get lost? They always follow the punchline.

How do you organize a comedy show? You plan-et.

Why did the comedian go to school? To improve his delivery.

Why don't some comedians ever get tired? They always have a good joke to tell.

What do you call a comedian that tells jokes? A pun-derful entertainer.

Why was the comedian always calm? He knew how to stay cool under pressure.

What's a comedian's favorite type of music? Stand-up rock.

Why did the comedian bring a ladder to the stage? To reach new heights.

How do you make a comedian laugh? Tell them a funny bone joke.

Why did the comedian stay at the spa? To get a little extra relaxation.

What do you call a lazy comedian? A slack-tivist.

Why don't some comedians play sports? They're afraid of dropping the punchline.

How do you keep a comedian from getting lost? Use a joke map.

What's a comedian's favorite game? Punchline Pursuit.

Why did the comedian go to therapy? He had too many issues to juggle.

What's a comedian's favorite book? The Comedy Bible.

Why was the comedian so confident? He knew he was always on top of his game.

How do you make a comedian dance? Put a little boogie in it.

Why did the comedian bring a map to the show? To find his way.

What do you call a comedian with no patience? A slow jokester.

Why did the comedian go to the doctor? He wasn't feeling too humorous.

What's a comedian's favorite movie? Funny People.

Why did the comedian go on a diet? To stay in shape for the stage.

What do you call a comedian who loves to sing? A crooner.

Competition Jokes

Why did the scarecrow win the competition? He was outstanding in his field.

Why don't some competitors get lost? They always follow the race.

How do you organize a competition? You plan-et.

Why don't some competitions ever get boring? They always have excitement.

What do you call a competition that tells jokes? A pun-test.

Why was the competitor always calm? They knew how to stay focused.

What's a competitor's favorite type of music? Competitive beats.

Why did the competitor bring a ladder to the contest? To reach new heights.

How do you make a competitor laugh? Tell them a victory joke.

Why did the competitor stay at the spa? To get a little extra relaxation.

What do you call a lazy competitor? A slack-tition.

Why don't some competitions ever get tiring? They always have challenges.

How do you keep a competitor from getting lost? Use a race map.

What's a competitor's favorite game? Capture the flag.

Why did the competitor go to therapy? They had too many unresolved issues.

What's a competitor's favorite book? The Art of Competition.

Why was the competitor so confident? They knew they were always on top.

How do you make a competitor dance? Put a little boogie in it.

Why did the competitor bring a map to the race? To find their way.

What do you call a competitor with no patience? A slow racer.

Why did the competitor go to the doctor? They weren't feeling too competitive.

What's a competitor's favorite movie? The Hunger Games.

Why did the competitor go on a diet? To stay fit for the race.

What do you call a competitor who loves to sing? A victory crooner.

Computer Jokes

Why did the computer go to art school? It wanted to learn to draw pixels.

Contemporary Jokes

Why don't scientists trust atoms? Because they make up everything!

How does a penguin build its house? Igloos it together.

What do you call fake spaghetti? An impasta!

What's orange and sounds like a parrot? A carrot.

I would tell you a construction joke, but I'm still working on it.

What do you call a can opener that doesn't work?

Crime Jokes

Why did the scarecrow become a great detective? He was outstanding in his field.

Why don't criminals ever get lost? They always follow the crime scene.

How do you organize a heist? You plan-et.

Why don't some criminals ever get tired? They always have energy for mischief.

What do you call a detective that tells jokes? A pun-detective.

Why was the criminal always calm? He knew how to stay grounded.

What's a detective's favorite type of music? Blues.

Why did the thief bring a ladder to the heist? To reach new heights.

How do you make a detective laugh? Tell them a clue-ver joke.

Why did the suspect stay at the spa? To get a little extra relaxation.

What do you call a lazy criminal? A slack-burglar.

Why don't some detectives play sports? They're afraid of missing clues.

How do you keep a detective from getting lost? Use a crime map.

What's a detective's favorite game? Clue.

Why did the criminal go to therapy? He had too many issues.

What's a detective's favorite book? The Hound of the Baskervilles.

Why was the detective so confident? He knew he was always on solid ground.

How do you make a detective dance? Put a little boogie in it.

Why did the detective bring a map to the case? To find his way.

What do you call a criminal with no patience? A slow-thief.

Why did the criminal go to the doctor? He wasn't feeling too well.

What's a detective's favorite movie? Sherlock Holmes.

Why did the criminal go on a diet? To stay fit for his getaways.

What do you call a detective who loves to sing? A clue-melody.

Dad Jokes

I only know 25 letters of the alphabet. I don't know y.

What do you call fake spaghetti? An impasta.

I would avoid the sushi if I was you. It's a little fishy.

I used to play piano by ear, but now I use my hands.

What do you call a factory that makes okay products? A satisfactory.

Did you hear about the cheese factory that exploded? There was nothing left but de-brie.

I'm reading a book on anti-gravity. It's impossible to put down.

What do you call a pile of cats? A meowtain.

Why did the golfer bring two pairs of pants? In case he got a hole in one.

Dance Jokes

Why don't dancers ever get lost? They always follow the rhythm.

How do you organize a dance party? You plan-et.

Why did the dancer go to school? To improve her moves.

Why don't some dancers ever get tired? They always have the energy.

What do you call a dancer that tells jokes? A pun-derella.

Why was the choreographer always calm? She knew how to stay grounded.

What's a dancer's favorite type of music? Anything with a good beat.

Why did the dancer bring a ladder to the studio? To reach new heights.

How do you make a dancer laugh? Tell them a toe-tapping joke.

Why did the dancer stay at the spa? To get a little extra relaxation.

What do you call a lazy dancer? A slack-stepper.

Why don't some dancers play sports? They're afraid of missing a step.

How do you keep a dancer from getting lost? Use a dance map.

What's a dancer's favorite game? Dance Dance Revolution.

Why did the dancer go to therapy? She had too many unresolved issues.

What's a dancer's favorite book? Ballet Shoes.

Why was the dancer so confident? She knew she was always in step.

How do you make a dancer dance? Put a little boogie in it.

Why did the dancer bring a map to the recital? To find her way.

What do you call a dancer with no patience? A slow-shuffle.

Why did the dancer go to the doctor? She wasn't feeling too well.

What's a dancer's favorite movie? Step Up.

Why did the dancer go on a diet? To stay light on her feet.

What do you call a dancer who loves to sing? A mel-stepper.

How do you make a ballerina cry? Tell her a sad plié story.

Dinosaur Jokes

Why don't dinosaurs ever get lost? Because they always stick to the Jurassic path.

How do you organize a dinosaur party? You plan-et.

Why did the dinosaur go to school? To become a little more dino-mite.

Why don't some dinosaurs ever get tired? Because they're always roaring.

What do you call a dinosaur that tells jokes? A pun-o-saurus.

Why was the dinosaur always calm? It knew how to stay grounded.

What's a dinosaur's favorite type of music? Rock and roar.

Why did the dinosaur bring a ladder to the park? To reach new heights.

How do you make a dinosaur laugh? Tell it a dino-mite joke.

Why did the dinosaur stay at the spa? To get a little extra relaxation.

What do you call a lazy dinosaur? A dino-snore.

Why don't some dinosaurs play sports? They're afraid of the roar-rivalry.

How do you keep a dinosaur from getting lost? Use a Jurassic map.

What's a dinosaur's favorite game? Hide and roar.

Why did the dinosaur go to therapy? It had too many issues.

What's a dinosaur's favorite book? How Do Dinosaurs Say Goodnight?

Why was the dinosaur so confident? It knew it was always on solid ground.

How do you make a dinosaur dance? Put a little boogie in it.

Why did the dinosaur bring a map to the adventure? To find its way.

What do you call a dinosaur with no patience? A slow-ris.

Why did the dinosaur go to the doctor? It wasn't feeling too well.

What's a dinosaur's favorite movie? Jurassic Park.

Why did the dinosaur go on a diet? To stay healthy.

What do you call a dinosaur who loves to sing? A dino-melody.

How do you organize a dinosaur race? You set the pterodactyl.

Doctor Jokes

Doctor, doctor, I feel like a pair of curtains! Pull yourself together!

I told my doctor I broke my arm in two places. He told me to stop going to those places.

Doctor, doctor, I swallowed a bone! Are you choking? No, I really did!

I went to the doctor with a sore throat. He gave me some tablets and told me to take them on an empty stomach. After that, I couldn't keep my appointment.

Doctor, doctor, I feel like a bridge! What's come over you? Two cars and a bus!

The doctor said I have type A blood, but it was a Type-O.

Doctor, doctor, my hair keeps falling out! Can you give me something to keep it in? Yes, a paper bag!

Doctor, doctor, I've only got 59 seconds to live! Hang on, I'll be with you in a minute.

Why did the doctor carry a red pen? In case they needed to draw blood.

Doctor, doctor, I feel like a spoon! Sit there and don't stir.

What did the doctor say to the rocket ship? Time to get your booster shot!

Doctor, doctor, I think I'm a bell! Take these pills and if they don't work, give me a ring.

Doctor, doctor, everyone keeps ignoring me! Next, please!

Why did the doctor take up art? He wanted to draw blood.

Doctor, doctor, I can't stop singing 'The Green, Green Grass of Home.' Sounds like Tom Jones Syndrome. Is it common? It's not unusual.

Doctor, doctor, I've got a strawberry stuck in my ear! Don't worry, I've got some cream for that.

Doctor, doctor, I keep thinking I'm a dog! How long have you had this feeling? Ever since I was a puppy.

Doctor, doctor, I can't feel my legs! I know, I amputated your arms.

Doctor, doctor, I think I'm invisible! Who said that?

Doctor, doctor, I feel like a deck of cards! I'll deal with you later.

Doctor, doctor, I've lost my memory! When did this happen? When did what happen?

Doctor, doctor, I have a serious problem. I can never remember what I just said. When did this start? When did what start?

Doctor, doctor, people keep telling me I'm a wheelbarrow. Don't let people push you around.

Why did the doctor get mad? He ran out of patients.

Doctor, doctor, I'm shrinking! You'll just have to be a little patient.

Fairy Tale Jokes

Why did Cinderella get kicked off the soccer team? Because she kept running away from the ball.

Why don't fairy tale characters get lost? They always follow the story.

How do you organize a fairy tale ball? You plan-et.

Why did the princess go to school? To improve her royal knowledge.

Why don't fairy tale characters ever get tired? They always live happily ever after.

What do you call a fairy tale character that tells jokes? A pun-celot.

Why was the prince always calm? He knew how to stay grounded.

What's a fairy tale character's favorite type of music? Enchanted melodies.

Why did the knight bring a ladder to the castle? To reach new heights.

How do you make a fairy tale character laugh? Tell them a magical joke.

Why did the fairy stay at the spa? To get a little extra relaxation.

What do you call a lazy fairy tale character? A couch knight.

Why don't fairy tale characters play sports? They're afraid of breaking the spell.

How do you keep a fairy tale character from getting lost? Use a story map.

What's a fairy tale character's favorite game? Hide and seek.

Why did the dragon go to therapy? It had too many issues.

What's a fairy tale character's favorite book? Grimm's Fairy Tales.

Why was the fairy tale character so confident? They knew they were always on solid ground.

How do you make a fairy tale character dance? Put a little boogie in it.

Why did the prince bring a map to the adventure? To find his way.

What do you call a fairy tale character with no patience? A slow prince.

Why did the princess go to the doctor? She wasn't feeling too well.

What's a fairy tale character's favorite movie? Tangled.

Why did the fairy tale character go on a diet? To stay in shape.

What do you call a fairy tale character who loves to sing? An enchanted melody.

Fantasy Jokes

Why don't wizards use computers? They prefer spell books.

Why don't fantasy characters get lost? They always follow the map.

How do you organize a fantasy quest? You plan-et.

Why don't some wizards ever get tired? They always have magic energy.

What do you call a fantasy character that tells jokes? A pun-icorn.

Why was the elf always calm? He knew how to stay grounded.

What's a fantasy character's favorite type of music? Mythical melodies.

Why did the dragon bring a ladder to the lair? To reach new heights.

How do you make a fantasy character laugh? Tell them a magical joke.

Why did the elf stay at the spa? To get a little extra relaxation.

What do you call a lazy fantasy character? A couch knight.

Why don't some wizards play sports? They're afraid of breaking the rules.

How do you keep a fantasy character from getting lost? Use a quest map.

What's a fantasy character's favorite game? Dungeons & Dragons.

What's a fantasy character's favorite book? The Lord of the Rings.

Why was the fantasy character so confident? They knew they were always on solid ground.

How do you make a fantasy character dance? Put a little boogie in it.

Why did the knight bring a map to the adventure? To find his way.

What do you call a fantasy character with no patience? A slow elf.

Why did the wizard go to the doctor? He wasn't feeling too well.

What's a fantasy character's favorite movie? The Princess Bride.

Why did the fantasy character go on a diet? To stay in shape.

What do you call a fantasy character who loves to sing? A mythical melody.

Fashion Jokes

Why did the scarecrow become a successful fashion model? He was outstanding in his field.

Why did the belt get arrested? For holding up the pants.

Why did the fashion designer go to jail? For too many patterns.

Why did the shoe go to school? To learn how to tie the knot.

Why don't skeletons wear clothes? Because they have no body to dress.

Why did the shirt go to the party? It wanted to button up.

Why did the fashion model bring string to the runway? To tie up loose ends.

What do you call a fashionable frog? A hop couture.

Why did the fashion show cross the road? To get to the other style.

Why did the tie go to the bar? To loosen up.

What's a shoe's favorite type of music? Sole.

Why did the pants go to therapy? They had too many issues.

Why don't some clothes play hide and seek? Because they're always getting worn out.

Why did the hat go to school? To get a little ahead.

Why don't shoes like to party? They don't like to get tied up.

Why did the scarecrow wear a new outfit? He wanted to impress the crows.

Why did the dress go to the party? It wanted to get a little style.

Why did the glasses go to school? To improve their vision.

Why did the fashion designer get a job at the bakery? To make some dough.

Why don't some clothes like the dryer? Because they get too heated.

What's a fashion designer's favorite fruit? A dress-berry.

Why did the shirt get promoted? It buttoned up and did its job.

Why did the jacket go to the party? To get zipped up.

Why don't some clothes like the hanger? Because they get hung up.

Why did the shoe go to the gym? To get a little sole training.

Festival Jokes

Why did the scarecrow join the festival? He was outstanding in his field.

Why don't some festival goers get lost? They always follow the music.

How do you organize a festival? You plan-et.

Why did the performer go to school? To improve his stage presence.

Why don't some festival rides ever get tired? They always have ups and downs.

What do you call a festival worker that tells jokes? A pun-festival.

Why was the festival organizer always calm? He knew how to stay grounded.

What's a festival's favorite type of music? Festival anthems.

Why did the performer bring a ladder to the stage? To reach new heights.

How do you make a festival goer laugh? Tell them a crowd-pleaser joke.

Why did the festival vendor stay at the spa? To get a little extra relaxation.

What do you call a lazy festival worker? A slack-fester.

Why don't some festival games ever get boring? They always have prizes.

How do you keep a festival goer from getting lost? Use a festival map.

What's a festival worker's favorite game? Dunk tank.

Why did the festival goer go to therapy? They had too many unresolved fun issues.

What's a festival worker's favorite book? The Festival of Insignificance.

Why was the festival performer so confident? He knew he was always on top of the show.

How do you make a festival worker dance? Put a little boogie in it.

Why did the festival worker bring a map to the fairgrounds? To find their way.

What do you call a festival goer with no patience? A slow reveler.

What's a festival worker's favorite movie? Woodstock.

Why did the festival vendor go on a diet? To stay fit for the food stands.

What do you call a festival worker who loves to sing? A tune-spinner.

Fishing Jokes

Why don't fish play piano? Because you can't tuna fish.

Why did the scarecrow become a great fisherman? He was outstanding in his field.

How do you organize a fishing trip? You plan-et.

What's a fish's favorite musical instrument? The bass guitar.

Why did the fish blush? Because it saw the ocean's bottom.

Why do fish never do well in school? Because they're always below sea level.

Why don't fish like computers? They're afraid of the net.

Why did the fish go to school? To improve its fin-telligence.

How do you make a fish laugh? Tell it a whale of a tale.

Why did the fisherman break up with the fish? It was too finicky.

What do you call a lazy fish? A slobberfish.

Why did the fish stay at the spa? To get a little extra relaxation.

Why don't fish play football? They're afraid of the tackle.

How do you keep a fish from smelling? Cut off its nose.

Why did the fisherman bring a ladder to the lake? To catch some high-flying fish.

What's a fish's favorite game? Scale-ot cards.

Why was the fish always calm? It knew how to go with the flow.

Why did the fish stay at the beach? Because it didn't want to be a fish out of water.

How do you organize a fishing party? You throw it on the line.

Why did the fisherman bring a pencil to the boat? To draw his line.

What's a fish's favorite movie? The Codfather.

Why was the fish so confident? It knew it was always in good water.

Why did the fish go to the doctor? It wasn't feeling fin-tastic.

What's a fish's favorite book? Catch-22.

Fitness Jokes

Why did the scarecrow become a successful athlete? He was outstanding in his field.

Why don't some people play hide and seek? Good luck hiding from their fitness goals.

Why did the gym close down? It just didn't work out.

Why don't some people go to the gym? They're already in great shape.

How do you organize a fitness party? You plan-et.

Why did the runner bring a pencil to the race? In case he needed to draw a tie.

Why did the yoga teacher bring string to class? To tie up loose ends.

Why did the weightlifter go to the beach? To work on his tan.

How does a cow stay fit? It goes to the moo-scles.

Why did the bicycle fall over? It was two-tired.

Why don't eggs go to the gym? They're afraid they'll crack up.

Why did the runner break up with the treadmill? It wasn't going anywhere.

Why did the boxer bring string to the ring? To tie up the competition.

Why did the weightlifter bring a ladder to the gym? To reach new heights.

What's a fitness enthusiast's favorite part of the computer? The hard drive.

How do cows stay fit? They run on the moo-dmill.

Why was the math book sad at the gym? It had too many problems to work out.

Why do marathon runners go broke? Because they run out of money.

Why don't some people lift weights at the gym? Because they prefer lifting their spirits.

Why did the fitness trainer go to art school? To learn how to draw abs.

What do you call a person who hates running but loves donuts? A fitness contradiction.

Why did the runner go to therapy? To get over his hurdles.

Food Jokes

Why did the tomato turn red? Because it saw the salad dressing!

How do you fix a broken tomato? With tomato paste.

What do you call a fake noodle? An impasta.

Why did the banana go to the doctor? Because it wasn't peeling well.

What do you call a sad strawberry? A blueberry.

Why did the grape stop in the middle of the road? Because it ran out of juice.

Why did the cookie go to the doctor? Because it felt crumby.

What did the lettuce say to the celery? Quit stalking me!

Why don't eggs tell jokes? They'd crack each other up.

What do you call a mischievous egg? A practical yolker.

Why did the mushroom go to the party alone? Because he's a fungi!

How do you make a lemon drop? Just let it fall.

What do you get when you cross a snowman and a vampire? Frostbite.

Why do watermelons have fancy weddings? Because they cantaloupe.

What does a nosy pepper do? Gets jalapeño business!

Put a little boogie in it.

What did the grape do when it got stepped on? Nothing, it just let out a little wine!

Why did the scarecrow win an award? Because he was outstanding in his field!

Why did the apple stop? Because it ran out of juice.

Friendship Jokes

Why did the scarecrow become a great friend? He was outstanding in his field.

Why don't some friends ever get lost? Because they always stick together.

How do you organize a friendship party? You plan-et.

Why did the friend go to school? To learn how to be a better buddy.

Why don't some friends ever get tired? Because they're always having fun.

What do you call a friend that tells jokes? A pun-derful pal.

Why were the friends always calm? They knew how to stay grounded.

What's a friend's favorite type of music? Friendship anthems.

Why did the friends bring a ladder to the adventure? To reach new heights together.

How do you make a friend laugh? Tell them a buddy-friendly joke.

Why did the friends stay at the spa? To get a little extra relaxation.

What do you call a lazy friend? A slack-pal.

Why don't some friends play sports? They're afraid of the rivalry.

How do you keep a friend from getting lost? Use a friendship map.

What's a friend's favorite game? Partner tag.

Why did the friends go to therapy? They had too many issues.

What's a friend's favorite book? Harry Potter and the Sorcerer's Stone.

Why were the friends so confident? They knew they were always on solid ground.

How do you make a friend dance? Put a little boogie in it.

Why did the friends bring a map to the adventure? To find their way together.

What do you call a friend with no patience? A slow buddy.

Why did the friends go to the doctor? They weren't feeling too well.

What's a friend's favorite movie? Toy Story.

Why did the friends go on a diet? To stay healthy together.

What do you call friends who love to sing? A harmony.

Game Show Jokes

Why did the scarecrow join the game show? He was outstanding in his field.

Why don't some contestants get lost? They always follow the host.

How do you organize a game show? You plan-et.

Why don't some game shows ever get boring? They always have questions.

What do you call a game show that tells jokes? A pun-show.

Why was the game show host always calm? They knew how to stay in control.

What's a contestant's favorite type of music? Quiz tunes.

Why did the contestant bring a ladder to the set? To reach new heights.

How do you make a game show contestant laugh? Tell them a winning joke.

What do you call a lazy contestant? A slack-quizzer.

Why don't some game shows ever get tiring? They always have prizes.

How do you keep a contestant from getting lost? Use a show map.

What's a game show's favorite game? Jeopardy.

What's a game show's favorite book? The Quiz Book.

Why did the contestant bring a map to the studio? To find their way.

What do you call a contestant with no patience? A slow buzzer.

Why did the contestant go to the doctor? They weren't feeling too quizzical.

What's a game show's favorite movie? Quiz Show.

Why did the contestant go on a diet? To stay fit for the show.

What do you call a game show contestant who loves to sing? A quiz crooner.

Gaming Jokes

Why don't some fish play video games? Because they're afraid of getting hooked.

Why did the gamer sit on the clock? Because he wanted to play time's up.

Why did the console go to therapy? It had too many issues.

Why did the scarecrow become a great gamer? He was outstanding in his field.

How do you organize a gaming party? You plan-et.

Why was the computer so good at gaming? It had all the right components.

Why did the gamer bring a ladder to the tournament? To reach the next level.

What's a gamer's favorite type of music? Chiptunes.

Why did the game developer go broke? Because he lost his assets.

Why did the video game player break up with the console? It found it too controlling.

Why don't some video games ever end? Because they always have a sequel.

Why did the joystick go to school? To improve its control.

Why did the game cartridge go to the doctor? It wasn't feeling too well.

What's a gamer's favorite type of bread? A high score.

Why did the scarecrow win the gaming tournament? He was outstanding in his field.

Why don't some gamers play hide and seek? Because good luck hiding from the screen.

Why did the video game go to school? To get a little smarter.

Why did the gamer bring string to the party? To tie up loose ends.

What do you call a video game about gardening? Plant-tendo.

Why did the controller go to the gym? To work on its grip.

Why don't skeletons play video games? They don't have the guts.

Why did the console go on a diet? It wanted to lose some bytes.

Why did the gamer take a nap? To save his progress.

What's a gamer's favorite type of shoes? Sneakers, for that fast run.

Why did the video game character bring a suitcase? Because it was going on a quest.

Gardening Jokes

Why was the gardener so calm? Because he knew how to weed out the stress.

What's a gardener's favorite type of music? Heavy mulch.

Why did the scarecrow become a gardener? He was outstanding in his field.

How do you organize a garden party? You plan-et.

Why did the gardener bring a ladder to the garden? To reach the high points.

Why don't some flowers ever get lost? Because they always follow the sun.

What do you call a lazy gardener? A couch potato.

Why was the tomato blushing? Because it saw the salad dressing.

What do you call a garden that's always on time? A punctual plot.

Why did the gardener go to therapy? To get over his garden issues.

Why don't some gardeners tell secrets? Because they might get spilled.

Why did the seed go to school? To improve its crop-abilities.

Why did the gardener bring string to the garden? To tie up loose ends.

Why was the garden always calm? Because it knew how to chill.

Why did the gardener go to the beach? To catch some rays.

What's a gardener's favorite game? Plant the flag.

Why did the carrot break up with the radish? It found it too rooted in its ways.

What do you call a garden that tells jokes? A plot twist.

Why did the gardener stay at the spa? To get a little extra mulch relaxation.

How do you make a garden laugh? Tell it a corny joke.

Why did the gardener bring a map to the garden? To find his way.

What's a gardener's favorite book? The Secret Garden.

Why did the gardener go to the doctor? He was feeling a little green.

Why was the garden so confident? It knew it was always in good soil.

Geography Jokes

Why was the geography book so smart? It had all the right coordinates.

Why don't mountains get cold in the winter? They wear snowcaps.

What's a geographer's favorite animal? A map turtle.

Why did the geography teacher go to the beach? To study the current events.

What's the capital of Alaska? Juneau.

Why did the map always excel in school? Because it had all the directions.

How do oceans say hello? They wave.

Why was the map bad at school? It lost all its places.

What do you call an educated globe? A sphere of influence.

Why did the geography student break up with the calculus book? It was too many problems.

What did the volcano say to the mountain? I lava you.

Why are geography teachers always tired? Because they have too many regions to cover.

What did the ocean say to the beach? Nothing, it just waved.

Why don't maps ever get lost? They always know where they stand.

Why did the compass go to school? To find its direction.

What do you call a lazy mountain? A slope.

Why was the geography book so confident? It knew the world inside out.

What's a geographer's favorite place to vacation? The top of the world.

Why did the river go to school? It wanted to improve its current.

Why do continents never get lost? They always stay in place.

What's a geographer's favorite kind of music? Country.

Why don't mountains get cold? Because they have snow caps.

Why was the map excited for vacation? It had all the right spots.

Why did the scarecrow become a geographer? He was outstanding in his field.

Ghost Jokes

Why don't ghosts ever get lost? Because they always follow the boo-levard.

How do you organize a ghost party? You plan-et.

Why did the ghost go to school? To improve its ghostly knowledge.

Why don't some ghosts ever get tired? Because they're always haunting.

What do you call a ghost that tells jokes? A pun-kin.

Why was the ghost always calm? It knew how to stay grounded.

What's a ghost's favorite type of music? Haunting melodies.

Why did the ghost bring a ladder to the haunted house? To reach new heights.

How do you make a ghost laugh? Tell it a spooky joke.

Why did the ghost stay at the spa? To get a little extra relaxation.

What do you call a lazy ghost? A couch boo-tato.

Why don't some ghosts play sports? They're afraid of the spirit competition.

How do you keep a ghost from getting lost? Use a spirit map.

What's a ghost's favorite game? Hide and shriek.

Why did the ghost go to therapy? It had too many issues.

What's a ghost's favorite book? The Ghost Whisperer.

Why was the ghost so confident? It knew it was always on solid ground.

How do you make a ghost dance? Put a little boogie in it.

Why did the ghost bring a map to the adventure? To find its way.

What do you call a ghost with no patience? A slow-ly spirit.

Why did the ghost go to the doctor? It wasn't feeling too well.

What's a ghost's favorite movie? Casper.

Why did the ghost go on a diet? To stay healthy.

What do you call a ghost who loves to sing? A boo-melody.

How do you organize a ghost race? You set the spook.

Graduation Jokes

Why did the scarecrow graduate with honors? He was outstanding in his field.

Why don't some graduates get lost? They always follow the commencement.

How do you organize a graduation ceremony? You plan-et.

Why did the student go to school? To improve their future prospects.

Why don't some graduates ever get tired? They always have a degree of energy.

What do you call a graduate that tells jokes? A pun-duate.

Why was the graduate always calm? They knew how to stay cool under pressure.

What's a graduate's favorite type of music? Pomp and Circumstance.

Why did the graduate bring a ladder to the stage? To reach new heights.

How do you make a graduate laugh? Tell them a commencement joke.

Why did the graduate stay at the spa? To get a little extra relaxation.

What do you call a lazy graduate? A slack-uate.

Why don't some graduates ever get boring? They always have future plans.

How do you keep a graduate from getting lost? Use a campus map.

What's a graduate's favorite game? Trivia Pursuit.

Why did the graduate go to therapy? They had too many unresolved issues.

What's a graduate's favorite book? Oh, the Places You'll Go!

Why was the graduate so confident? They knew they were always the main event.

How do you make a graduate dance? Put a little boogie in it.

Why did the graduate bring a map to the ceremony? To find their way.

What do you call a graduate with no patience? A slow learner.

Why did the graduate go to the doctor? They weren't feeling too well-educated.

What's a graduate's favorite movie? Legally Blonde.

Why did the graduate go on a diet? To stay fit for the future.

What do you call a graduate who loves to sing? A commencement crooner.

Health Jokes

Why did the scarecrow go to the doctor? He was outstanding in his field.

Why did the doctor bring a pencil to work? To draw blood.

Why don't some doctors trust stairs? They're always up to something.

Why don't skeletons fight each other? They don't have the guts.

How do you organize a healthy party? You kale it.

Why did the doctor sit on the needle? He wanted to be on point.

Why did the grape go to the hospital? Because it was feeling vine.

Why did the health teacher go to jail? Because he had too many vitamins.

Why did the apple go to school? To get a little smarter.

Why did the computer take a nap? It needed to reboot.

Why did the scarecrow become a doctor? He was outstanding in his field.

Why was the math book sad at the hospital? It had too many problems to solve.

Why don't some people eat clocks? Because it's time-consuming.

Why did the doctor sit on his watch? He wanted to be on time.

Why don't some people like to talk to vegetables? They don't carrot all.

Why did the fitness trainer go to therapy? To work out his issues.

Why did the patient sit on a pencil? Because it was a point to discuss.

Why did the nurse carry a red pen? In case she needed to draw blood.

Hiking Jokes

Why don't mountains get cold? They wear snow caps.

How do you organize a hiking trip? You plan-et.

What did the mountain climber name his son? Cliff.

Why did the scarecrow become a hiker? He was outstanding in his field.

What's a hiker's favorite type of music? Rock and roll.

Why don't some hikers get lost? They always follow the trail mix.

What do you call a lazy hiker? A trail potato.

Why was the mountain always calm? It knew how to stay grounded.

How do mountains see? They peak.

Why did the hiker bring a ladder? To reach new heights.

Why don't some hikers ever get bored? Because they're always in-tents.

What do you call a mountain that tells jokes? A hill-arious.

Why did the mountain go to therapy? It had a lot of peaks and valleys.

What's a hiker's favorite drink? Mountain Dew.

Why did the hiker bring a pencil to the trail? To draw a map.

How do you make a hiker laugh? Tell it a trail of a joke.

Why did the hiker stay at the spa? To get a little extra relaxation.

What's a hiker's favorite game? Capture the peak.

Why did the hiker go to the beach? To get some rays.

Why was the mountain so confident? It knew it was always on solid ground.

What do you call a hiker who loves math? An alge-brain.

Why did the hiker go to the library? To check out the great outdoors.

How do you make a mountain laugh? Tell it a rocky joke.

Why did the hiker bring a book to the trail? To catch up on some reading.

What's a hiker's favorite book? Where the Wild Things Are.

Historical Jokes

Why was the math book sad during history class? It had too many dates.

Why did the history book look so smart? It was full of dates.

Why don't you find history majors at the beach? They're afraid of the dates.

Why did the Roman stay out of the sun? He didn't want to be tan.

Why did the scarecrow become a great philosopher? He was outstanding in his field.

How did the ancient Egyptians talk to each other? They used hieroglyphics.

Why did the historian cross the road? To get to the other century.

Why did the history teacher bring a ladder to class? To show the students the high points.

Why did George Washington have trouble sleeping? Because he couldn't lie.

Why was the medieval knight always calm? Because he had a lot of inner peas.

How do you know Abraham Lincoln was honest? He never lied.

Why did the history book go to school? To improve its knowledge of the past.

Why was the archaeologist always calm? Because he had a lot of patience.

What do you call a medieval spy? A knight-stalker.

Why did the scarecrow become a successful leader? He was outstanding in his field.

What did one pyramid say to the other? Stop trying to be a tomb copy.

Why did the ancient Greeks never get lost? They always had their city-states.

Why did the historian eat his notes? Because he wanted to digest the past.

Why was the Civil War so lit? Because it had a lot of cannon balls.

Why did the Renaissance start in Italy? Because the pasta was worth fighting for.

Why did the knight run for president? He wanted to lead the charge.

Why did the explorer take a map to bed? He wanted to get a good night's sleep.

Why did the scarecrow get a Nobel Prize? He was outstanding in his field.

What do you call a medieval mathematician? A knight in shining numerals.

Why did the king go to the dentist? To get his crown checked.

Holiday Jokes

What do you get if you cross a snowman and a vampire? Frostbite.

Why was the math book sad over the holidays? Because it had too many problems.

Why do mummies like Christmas so much? Because of all the wrapping.

What do you call an elf who sings? A wrapper.

Why is it always cold at Christmas? Because it's in Decembrrr.

What kind of motorcycle does Santa ride? A Holly Davidson.

Why was the turkey at the Christmas party? Because it was stuffed.

How do you scare a snowman? You get a hairdryer.

Why did the skeleton not go to the New Year's Eve party? He had no body to go with.

Why did the turkey cross the road? To prove it wasn't a chicken.

What do Santa's helpers learn in school? The elf-abet.

Why do Christmas trees like the past? Because the present's beneath them.

What do you get when you cross a Christmas tree with an iPad? A pineapple.

Why did the Easter egg hide? Because it was a little chicken.

What did the beaver say to the Christmas tree? Nice gnawing you!

Why is Santa so good at karate? Because he has a black belt.

Why don't you ever see Santa in the hospital? Because he has private elf care.

Why did the scarecrow win an award? He was outstanding in his field.

What did one Christmas light say to the other? You light up my life.

What's Santa's favorite type of music? Wrap.

Why don't you eat Christmas decorations? Because you might get tinselitis.

What do you call a greedy elf? Elfish.

How does a snowman get around? By riding an "icicle."

What's a snowman's favorite snack? Ice crispy treats.

Holiday Season Jokes

Why did the scarecrow become a holiday decorator? He was outstanding in his field.

Why don't some people get lost during the holidays? They always follow the festive lights.

How do you organize a holiday party? You plan-et.

Why don't some reindeer ever get tired? They always have holiday spirit.

What do you call a holiday decorator that tells jokes? A pun-dolf.

Why was Santa always calm? He knew how to stay jolly.

What's a snowman's favorite type of music? Cool jazz.

Why did the reindeer bring a ladder to the workshop? To reach the rooftop.

How do you make a snowman laugh? Tell them a frosty joke.

Why did the gingerbread man stay at the spa? To get a little extra relaxation.

What do you call a lazy elf? A slack-santa.

Why don't some people play sports during the holidays? They're afraid of getting snowed under.

How do you keep a holiday enthusiast from getting lost? Use a festive map.

What's a snowman's favorite game? Freeze tag.

Why did the Christmas tree go to therapy? It had too many tangled lights.

What's an elf's favorite book? The Polar Express.

Why was the holiday season so confident? It knew it was always the most wonderful time of the year.

How do you make Santa dance? Put a little boogie in it.

Why did the snowman bring a map to the North Pole? To find his way.

What do you call a holiday grinch with no patience? A slow Grinch.

Why did the elf go to the doctor? He wasn't feeling too elfy.

What's Santa's favorite movie? Miracle on 34th Street.

Why did the snowman go on a diet? To stay frosty.

What do you call a reindeer who loves to sing? A carol-deer.

Impressionist Jokes

Why did the scarecrow become an impressionist? He was outstanding in his field.

Why don't some impressionists get lost? They always follow their mimicry.

How do you organize an impressionist show? You plan-et.

Why did the impressionist go to school? To improve his impersonations.

Why don't some impressionists ever get tired? They always have new characters to mimic.

What do you call an impressionist that tells jokes? A pun-mimic.

Why was the impressionist always calm? He knew how to stay in character.

What's an impressionist's favorite type of music? Voice-overs.

Why did the impressionist bring a ladder to the stage? To reach new heights.

How do you make an impressionist laugh? Tell them a mimicry joke.

Why did the impressionist stay at the spa? To get a little extra relaxation.

What do you call a lazy impressionist? A slack-actor.

Why don't some impressionists play sports? They're afraid of missing the cues.

How do you keep an impressionist from getting lost? Use a character map.

What's an impressionist's favorite game? Charades.

Why did the impressionist go to therapy? He had too many unresolved issues.

What's an impressionist's favorite book? The Art of Mimicry.

Why was the impressionist so confident? He knew he was always on top of his game.

How do you make an impressionist dance? Put a little boogie in it.

Why did the impressionist bring a map to the audition? To find his way.

What do you call an impressionist with no patience? A slow impersonator.

Why did the impressionist go to the doctor? He wasn't feeling too animated.

What's an impressionist's favorite movie? Dead Ringers.

Why did the impressionist go on a diet? To stay in shape for the role.

What do you call an impressionist who loves to sing? A mimic-melody.

Internet Jokes

Why did the scarecrow become a successful blogger? He was outstanding in his field.

Why did the computer go on the internet? To improve its net worth.

How do you know the ocean is friendly? It waves, even on the internet.

Why did the internet break up with the printer? Because it had too many paper jams.

Why don't some people ever get bored online? Because they're always surfing.

Why did the Wi-Fi go to the party? To make some connections.

Why did the web designer go broke? He lost his domain.

Why did the internet take a nap? Because it needed to refresh.

What's a computer's favorite dance? The internet hop.

Why did the email go to therapy? Because it had too many issues.

Why did the search engine go to school? To improve its browsing.

What do you call a website that's good at lying? A phish.

Why did the computer join the band? Because it had the best megabytes.

Why was the internet always calm? It had good bandwidth.

What's a computer's favorite place to go? The Web.

Why did the browser go to the party? To find some cookies.

Why was the internet so confident? It had a lot of cache.

Why did the computer go to the beach? To surf the web.

How do you organize an online party? You stream it.

Why don't some people like the internet? Because it's too webby.

What did one computer say to the other? "You're just my type."

Why did the computer go to the store? To get some new peripherals.

Why was the internet always so happy? It had lots of connections.

Why did the website go to therapy? It needed to work on its cookies.

Kids Jokes

Why did the student eat his homework? Because his teacher said it was a piece of cake.

Why did the math book look sad? Because it had too many problems.

Why did the bicycle fall over? Because it was two-tired.

Why was the music teacher arrested? Because she got caught with too many notes.

Why did the scarecrow win an award? Because he was outstanding in his field.

What did the zero say to the eight? Nice belt!

Why can't you give Elsa a balloon? Because she'll let it go.

Why did the tomato turn red? Because it saw the salad dressing.

What do you call a dog magician? A labracadabrador.

How do you catch a squirrel? Climb up in a tree and act like a nut.

Why do bananas never get lonely? Because they hang out in bunches.

Why did the frog take the bus to work? Because his car got toad.

Knock-Knock Jokes

Knock, knock.

Who's there?

Lettuce.

Lettuce who?

Lettuce in, it's freezing out here!

Boo.

Boo who?

Don't cry, it's just a joke!

Cow says.

Cow says who?

No, cow says moo!

Olive.

Olive who?

Olive you and I miss you!

Atch.

Atch who?

Bless you!

Harry.

Harry who?

Harry up and answer the door!

Tank.

Tank who?

You're welcome.

Alice.

Alice who?

Alice fair in love and war.

Orange.

Orange who?

Orange you going to let me in?

Dishes.

Dishes who?

Dishes the police, open up!

Broken pencil.

Broken pencil who?

Never mind, it's pointless.

Canoe.

Canoe who?

Canoe help me with my homework?

Doughnut.

Doughnut who?

Doughnut forget to give me a call!

Nobel.

Nobel who?

Nobel, that's why I knocked!

Leaf.

Leaf who?

Leaf me alone!

Dewey.

Dewey who?

Dewey have to keep doing this?

Peas.

Peas who?

Peas let me in!

Tish.

Tish who?

Tish the season to be jolly!

Honeydew.

Honeydew who?

Honeydew you love me?

Figs.

Figs who?

Figs the doorbell, it's broken!

A little old lady.

A little old lady who?

I didn't know you could yodel!

Butter.

Butter who?

Butter let me in or I'll freeze!

Snow.

Snow who?

Snow use, I forgot my key.

Ice cream.

Ice cream who?

Ice cream every time I see a scary movie!

Turner.

Turner who?

Turner round and let me see your face!

Lawyer Jokes

What's the difference between a lawyer and a herd of buffalo? The lawyer charges more.

Why don't sharks attack lawyers? Professional courtesy.

What's the difference between a lawyer and a leech? After you die, a leech stops sucking your blood.

How does an attorney sleep? First, he lies on one side, then he lies on the other side.

What do you call a lawyer who doesn't chase ambulances? Retired.

Why don't lawyers go to the beach? Cats keep trying to bury them in the sand.

What's the difference between a lawyer and a vulture? Lawyers accumulate frequent flyer miles.

What's the difference between a lawyer and a vampire? A vampire only sucks blood at night.

How many lawyers does it take to change a light bulb? How many can you afford?

What do honest lawyers and UFOs have in common? You always hear about them, but you never see them.

What's the difference between a lawyer and a boxing referee? A boxing referee doesn't get paid more for a longer fight.

What's the difference between a lawyer and a trampoline? You take off your shoes before you jump on a trampoline.

Why did the lawyer cross the road? To get to the car accident on the other side.

What's the difference between a lawyer and a skunk? One is a dirty, stinking, smelly beast, and the other is a skunk.

What do you get when you cross a lawyer with a demon from hell? No change at all.

How can you tell if a lawyer is lying? Other lawyers look interested.

What do you call 25 lawyers buried up to their chins in cement? Not enough cement.

What's the difference between a lawyer and a herd of cows? A lawyer charges more.

Why did the lawyer show up at the bar in a suit? Because he wanted to press charges.

What's the difference between a lawyer and a bucket of manure? The bucket.

What's the difference between a lawyer and a catfish? One is a scum-sucking bottom-dweller, and the other is a fish.

How do you save a drowning lawyer? Take your foot off his head.

Why don't lawyers read novels? The only numbers in them are page numbers.

What's the difference between a lawyer and a mosquito? One is a blood-sucking parasite, the other is an insect.

What do you get when you cross a lawyer with a pig? Nothing, there's some things a pig won't do.

Library Jokes

Why did the scarecrow become a librarian? He was outstanding in his field.

Why don't some books ever get lost? Because they always follow their pages.

Why did the library book go to therapy? Because it had too many issues.

What's a librarian's favorite kind of candy? Book-erface.

What did one book say to the other? "You're a real page-turner!"

Why don't some books play hide and seek? Because they're always getting read.

What do you call a library full of cats? A purr-suing library.

Why did the book go to the party? It wanted to get checked out.

Why don't some books play sports? Because they get too worn out.

Why did the library book go to the doctor? It had a spine problem.

What do you call a librarian who loves to dance? A book-shaker.

Why did the librarian always stay calm? Because she had a lot of patrons.

What's a librarian's favorite vegetable? Quiet peas.

Why did the library book join the band? Because it had great cover art.

Why did the librarian bring a ladder to work? To reach new heights in reading.

Why was the library so quiet? Because it had too many silent letters.

Why did the library book go on vacation? To get some shelf-care.

What's a librarian's favorite type of music? Reading rhythm.

Why did the librarian become a gardener? To weed out bad books.

What do you call a book with no pictures? A novel idea.

Why did the librarian bring string to the library? To tie up loose ends.

Light Bulb Jokes

How many software engineers does it take to change a light bulb? None. It's a hardware problem.

How many psychiatrists does it take to change a light bulb? Only one, but the light bulb has to want to change.

How many tickles does it take to make an octopus laugh? Ten-tickles.

How many actors does it take to change a light bulb? Only one. They don't like to share the spotlight.

How many narcissists does it take to change a light bulb? Just one. They hold the bulb while the world revolves around them.

How many pessimists does it take to change a light bulb? None. They just sit in the dark and moan about how bad the light is.

How many optimists does it take to change a light bulb? None. They're convinced the light will come back on by itself.

How many mystery writers does it take to change a light bulb? Two. One to screw it almost all the way in and the other to give it a surprising twist at the end.

How many dentists does it take to change a light bulb? One, but it takes several visits.

How many drummers does it take to change a light bulb? None. They have machines for that now.

How many magicians does it take to change a light bulb? Just one, but it'll disappear and reappear in someone's ear.

How many gym enthusiasts does it take to change a light bulb? One, but they'll do it after their next set.

How many chefs does it take to change a light bulb? None. They chop the bulb and serve it with garnish.

How many philosophers does it take to change a light bulb? It depends on how you interpret the act of changing.

How many quantum physicists does it take to change a light bulb? If you know the number, you can't be certain whether the bulb is changed.

How many gardeners does it take to change a light bulb? Three. One to change it and two to argue about whether it's a flower or a weed.

How many accountants does it take to change a light bulb? What kind of answer did you have in mind?

How many actors does it take to change a light bulb? None. They'll just stand in the dark, pretending they're in a dramatic scene.

How many lifeguards does it take to change a light bulb? None. They watch from a distance in case it gets screwed up.

How many software testers does it take to change a light bulb? None. They just report that the bulb is dark.

How many tech support staff does it take to change a light bulb? Have you tried turning it off and on again?

How many statisticians does it take to change a light bulb? One, plus or minus three.

How many actors does it take to change a light bulb? None. They'll just read the script and fake it.

How many social workers does it take to change a light bulb? None. They empower the light bulb to change itself.

How many writers does it take to change a light bulb? Just one, but it'll take forever to get it just right.

Magician Jokes

Why did the scarecrow become a magician? He was outstanding in his field.

Why don't some magicians get lost? They always follow the magic trick.

How do you organize a magic show? You plan-et.

Why did the magician go to school? To improve his sleight of hand.

Why don't some magicians ever get tired? They always have tricks up their sleeves.

What do you call a magician that tells jokes? A pun-caster.

Why was the magician always calm? He knew how to stay magical.

What's a magician's favorite type of music? Abracadabra tunes.

Why did the magician bring a ladder to the stage? To reach new heights.

How do you make a magician laugh? Tell them a trick joke.

Why did the magician stay at the spa? To get a little extra relaxation.

What do you call a lazy magician? A slack-ician.

Why don't some magicians play sports? They're afraid of dropping the ball.

How do you keep a magician from getting lost? Use a magic map.

What's a magician's favorite game? Illusion charades.

Why did the magician go to therapy? He had too many unresolved issues.

What's a magician's favorite book? The Magic of Reality.

Why was the magician so confident? He knew he was always on top of his game.

How do you make a magician dance? Put a little boogie in it.

Why did the magician bring a map to the show? To find his way.

What do you call a magician with no patience? A slow illusionist.

Why did the magician go to the doctor? He wasn't feeling too magical.

What's a magician's favorite movie? Now You See Me.

Why did the magician go on a diet? To stay in shape for the tricks.

What do you call a magician who loves to sing? An illusion-crooner.

Marriage Jokes

Why did the scarecrow become a great husband? He was outstanding in his field.

Why don't some marriages ever get lost? Because they always stay on course.

How do you organize a marriage? You plan-et.

Why did the couple go to school? To improve their relationship.

Why don't some couples ever get tired? Because they always stay together.

What do you call a marriage that tells jokes? A pun-derful.

Why was the marriage always calm? It knew how to stay grounded.

What's a couple's favorite type of music? Love songs.

Why did the couple bring a ladder to the ceremony? To reach new heights together.

How do you make a marriage laugh? Tell it a happily-ever-after joke.

Why did the couple stay at the spa? To get a little extra relaxation.

What do you call a lazy couple? A slack-duo.

Why don't some couples play sports? They're afraid of the arguments.

How do you keep a marriage from getting lost? Use a love map.

What's a couple's favorite game? Love and marriage.

Why did the couple go to therapy? They had too many issues.

What's a marriage's favorite book? Love Story.

Why was the marriage so confident? It knew it was always on solid ground.

How do you make a marriage dance? Put a little boogie in it.

Why did the couple bring a map to the journey? To find their way together.

What do you call a marriage with no trust? A slow relationship.

Why did the couple go to the doctor? They weren't feeling too well.

What's a couple's favorite movie? The Notebook.

Why did the couple go on a diet? To stay healthy together.

Math Jokes

Why was the equal sign so humble? Because it wasn't less than or greater than anyone else.

Why was the math book sad? Because it had too many problems.

Why do plants hate math? Because it gives them square roots.

Why was the fraction worried about marrying the decimal? Because he would have to convert.

What's a math teacher's favorite place in NYC? Times Square.

Why don't you do arithmetic in the jungle? Because if you add 4+4 you get ate!

How do you make seven even? Take away the "s."

What's a math teacher's favorite season? Sum-mer.

Why did the two fours skip lunch? They already eight.

Why did the student do multiplication problems on the floor? The teacher told him not to use tables.

Why didn't the quarter roll down the hill with the nickel? Because it had more cents.

What is a math teacher's favorite dessert? Pi.

What's the king of the pencil case? The ruler.

Why did the mathematician work at a bakery? Because he was good at pie charts.

How do you stay warm in a cold room? Just huddle in the corner, where it's always 90 degrees.

Why did the student wear glasses in math class? Because it improved di-vision.

How does a mathematician plow fields? With a pro-tractor.

Why was six afraid of seven? Because seven eight nine.

What did one math book say to the other? I've got problems.

What's a math teacher's favorite sum? Summer vacation.

Why did the obtuse angle go to the beach? Because it was over 90 degrees.

Why are obtuse angles so depressed? Because they're never right.

How do you solve any equation? Multiply both sides by zero.

What do you call an empty parrot cage? A polygon.

Why did the math teacher break up with the biology teacher? There was no chemistry.

Medical Jokes

What do you call a doctor who fixes websites? A URLologist.

Why did the computer go to the doctor? It had a virus.

Why did the nurse always carry a pencil? In case they needed to draw blood.

What do you call a funny bone doctor? A humerus.

Why did the patient sit on the clock? He wanted to be on time.

Why was the math book sad at the doctor's office? It had too many problems.

How does a doctor freshen her breath? With experi-mints.

Why did the skeleton go to the doctor? It had no body to go with.

Why did the doctor carry a ladder? To reach new heights in medicine.

Why don't some doctors ever get bored? Because they're always in stitches.

What do you call a doctor who fixes broken hearts? A cardiologist.

Why did the doctor take a nap? He needed to catch up on his zzz's.

What did the doctor say to the rocket ship? "Time for your booster shot!"

Why was the doctor always calm? Because he had a lot of patients.

Why did the computer sit in the doctor's office? It needed a check-up.

What do you get when you cross a doctor with a dog? A vet.

Why did the doctor bring a pencil to surgery? To draw conclusions.

What did one tonsil say to the other? "Get dressed, the doctor is taking us out!"

Movie Jokes

Why don't skeletons fight in movies? They don't have the guts.

What's a vampire's favorite movie? A bite film.

Why did the movie go to the hospital? It had a reel problem.

Why did the scarecrow become an actor? He was outstanding in his field.

What do you call a movie about cows? A moo-vie.

Why don't movie stars play hide and seek? Because good luck hiding in plain sight.

Why did the movie about pencils get bad reviews? It was pointless.

How do you organize a space movie party? You planet.

What's the best way to watch a fly movie? With insect repellent.

Why did the scarecrow become a film director? He was outstanding in his field.

Why did the tomato blush at the movie? It saw the salad dressing.

What's a ghost's favorite movie genre? Horror flicks.

Why did the popcorn go to the movies? It wanted to be a kernel star.

How does a vampire watch a movie? By biting through the scenes.

Why did the chicken join the movie? Because it wanted to be a cluck star.

What kind of movies do owls like? Hoo-dunnits.

Why did the film critic give up on writing? Because he couldn't find the right script.

Why was the movie about camping boring? It was too in-tents.

What do you get if you cross an actor with a vampire? A bloodthirsty performer.

What's a film producer's favorite food? A movie platter.

Why did the director use a ladder? To reach new heights in filmmaking.

What did the movie director say to the broken camera? "You're not on the scene anymore!"

Why did the film star go to the party? To celebrate their reel success.

Why are action movies so fast? They don't have time to slow down.

What's a pirate's favorite movie? Anything rated "Arrr!"

Music Jokes

Why did the music teacher go to jail? Because she got caught with the wrong notes.

How do you fix a broken tuba? With a tuba glue.

How do you make a tissue dance? Put a little boogie in it.

Why did the piano break up with the accordion? It found it too pushy.

Why did the scarecrow become a successful musician? He was outstanding in his field.

Why did Mozart get rid of his chickens? Because they kept saying "Bach, Bach!"

What's a skeleton's least favorite room in the house? The living room.

Why was the musician arrested? He got caught with too many notes.

Why did the guitar teacher go to jail? For fingering A minor.

What is Beethoven's favorite fruit? Ba-na-na-na.

What makes music on your head? A headband.

How do you make a bandstand? Take away their chairs.

Why couldn't the athlete listen to her music? Because she broke the record.

What's a balloon's least favorite type of music? Pop.

Why was the piano so hard to open? Because the keys were inside.

Why did the musician get kicked out of class? Because he couldn't keep his composure.

What kind of music are balloons afraid of? Pop music.

Why do cows make great musicians? Because they have great calves.

Why was the piano teacher arrested? She was caught with too many notes.

How does a singer say goodbye? So long, farewell, auf Wiedersehen, goodbye.

Why did the computer go to music school? It wanted to improve its memory.

What do you get if you cross a sweet potato and a jazz musician? A yam session.

Why was the orchestra so good? It had great conduct.

Mystery Jokes

Why did the detective bring a ladder to the crime scene? To get to the bottom of things.

Why don't mystery novels ever get lost? They always have a plot.

How do you organize a mystery party? You plan-et.

Why don't some detectives ever get tired? They're always on the case.

What do you call a detective that tells jokes? A pun-sleuth.

Why was the detective always calm? He knew how to stay grounded.

What's a detective's favorite type of music? Blues clues.

Why did the detective bring a flashlight to the crime scene? To shed some light on the subject.

How do you make a detective laugh? Tell them a mysterious joke.

Why did the detective stay at the spa? To relax and solve the case later.

What do you call a lazy detective? A slack-sleuth.

Why did the detective go to therapy? He had too many unresolved issues.

What do you call a detective with no patience? A slow-thinker.

Why did the detective go to the doctor? He wasn't feeling too well.

Why did the detective go on a diet? To stay fit for the chase.

Nature Jokes

Why don't trees use the internet? Because they log off.

Why don't flowers ride bikes? Because they lose their petals.

What did one ocean say to the other? Nothing, they just waved.

Why did the scarecrow become a great gardener? He was outstanding in his field.

What do you call a fish without an eye? Fsh.

Why did the tree go to the dentist? To get a root canal.

How do you cut a wave in half? Use a sea-saw.

Why don't mountains get cold in the winter? They wear snow caps.

Why are frogs so happy? Because they eat whatever bugs them.

What do you call a cow during an earthquake? A milkshake.

Why don't bees get lost? They always know their buzz-ness.

How does the ocean say hi? It waves.

Why do birds fly south for the winter? Because it's too far to walk.

Why are spiders great at the internet? They're great at catching bugs.

Why do fish always sing off-key? Because you can't tuna fish.

Why don't some trees use the internet? Because they're afraid of logging in.

Office Jokes

Why did the scarecrow become a successful office worker? He was outstanding in his field.

Why don't some employees play hide and seek? Because good luck hiding from emails.

What did one elevator say to the other? I think I'm coming down with something.

Why was the computer cold? It left its Windows open.

Why did the coffee file a police report? It got mugged.

Why did the office worker bring a ladder to work? Because he wanted to go to the next level.

Why did the employee get fired from the calendar factory? He took a few days off.

Why did the office worker bring a suitcase to work? Because he was checking in for a long day.

What did the janitor say when he jumped out of the closet? Supplies!

Why did the office worker sit on his watch? Because he wanted to be on time.

Why was the computer so smart? Because it had a lot of bytes.

Why don't programmers like nature? It has too many bugs.

Why did the paper file a complaint? Because it was getting folded unfairly.

What's a printer's favorite sport? Paper jams.

Why don't some employees eat at their desks? Because they don't want to work lunch overtime.

Why did the stapler break up with the paper? It couldn't hold it together anymore.

Why did the pen join the circus? It wanted to draw a crowd.

Why did the office worker join the band? Because he had great notes.

Why did the clock get a job? It wanted to make good time.

Parenting Jokes

Why did the scarecrow become a great parent? He was outstanding in his field.

Why don't some parents ever get lost? Because they always follow the family plan.

How do you organize a family trip? You plan-et.

Why don't some parents ever get tired? Because they always stay on top of things.

What do you call a parent that tells jokes? A pun-derful parent.

Why was the parent always calm? They knew how to stay grounded.

What's a parent's favorite type of music? Lullabies.

Why did the parent bring a ladder to the park? To reach new heights with their kids.

How do you make a parent laugh? Tell them a family-friendly joke.

Why did the parent stay at the spa? To get a little extra relaxation.

What do you call a lazy parent? A slack-dad or slack-mom.

Why don't some parents play sports? They're afraid of the tantrums.

How do you keep a parent from getting lost? Use a parenting map.

What's a parent's favorite game? Hide and seek.

Why did the parent go to therapy? They had too many parenting issues.

What's a parent's favorite book? Goodnight Moon.

Why was the parent so confident? They knew they were always on solid ground.

How do you make a parent dance? Put a little boogie in it.

Why did the parent bring a map to the journey? To find their way as a family.

What do you call a parent with no patience? A slow learner.

Why did the parent go to the doctor? They weren't feeling too well.

What's a parent's favorite movie? Finding Nemo.

Why did the parent go on a diet? To stay healthy for their kids.

What do you call a parent who loves to sing? A lullaby-er.

Pet Jokes

Why did the dog sit in the shade? Because it didn't want to be a hot dog.

Why did the scarecrow become a pet trainer? He was outstanding in his field.

Why don't some pets get lost? They always follow their noses.

How do you organize a pet show? You plan-et.

Why did the cat sit on the computer? To keep an eye on the mouse.

What do you call a pet that tells jokes? A pun-derful pet.

Why was the dog always calm? It knew how to stay pawsitive.

What's a pet's favorite type of music? Bark 'n' roll.

Why did the bird bring a ladder to the nest? To reach new heights.

How do you make a pet laugh? Tell it a funny bone joke.

What do you call a lazy pet? A couch pooch.

Why don't some pets play sports? They're afraid of the competition.

How do you keep a pet from getting lost? Use a pawprint map.

What's a pet's favorite game? Fetch.

Why did the hamster go to therapy? It had too many wheel issues.

What's a pet's favorite book? Clifford the Big Red Dog.

Why was the pet so confident? It knew it was always in good hands.

How do you make a pet dance? Put a little boogie in it.

Why did the pet bring a map to the park? To find its way.

What do you call a pet with no patience? A slowpoke.

Why did the rabbit go to the doctor? It wasn't feeling very hoppy.

What's a pet's favorite movie? The Secret Life of Pets.

Why did the pet go on a diet? To stay healthy.

What do you call a pet who loves to sing? A purrformer.

Photography Jokes

Why don't photographers ever get lost? They always follow the focus.

How do you organize a photo shoot? You plan-et.

Why did the photographer go to school? To improve his exposure.

Why don't some photographers ever get tired? They're always developing new ideas.

What do you call a photographer that tells jokes? A pun-tographer.

Why was the photographer always calm? He knew how to stay grounded.

What's a photographer's favorite type of music? Snap tunes.

Why did the photographer bring a ladder to the shoot? To get a better angle.

How do you make a photographer laugh? Tell them a picture-perfect joke.

Why did the photographer stay at the spa? To get a little extra relaxation.

What do you call a lazy photographer? A slack-shutter.

Why don't some photographers play sports? They're afraid of missing the shot.

How do you keep a photographer from getting lost? Use a photo map.

What's a photographer's favorite game? Snapshot.

Why did the photographer go to therapy? He had too many unresolved issues.

What's a photographer's favorite book? The Camera Never Blinks.

Why was the photographer so confident? He knew he was always in focus.

How do you make a photographer dance? Put a little boogie in it.

Why did the photographer bring a map to the shoot? To find the perfect spot.

What do you call a photographer with no patience? A slow-shutter.

Why did the photographer go to the doctor? He wasn't feeling too well.

What's a photographer's favorite movie? Shutter Island.

Why did the photographer go on a diet? To stay light on his feet.

What do you call a photographer who loves to sing? A snap-melody.

How do you make a photographer cry? Expose their negatives.

Pirate Jokes

Why don't pirates shower before they walk the plank? Because they'll just wash up on shore later.

What's a pirate's favorite letter? You might think it's R, but it's the C they truly love.

Why did the pirate go to school? To improve his arrr-ticulation.

How do pirates prefer to communicate? Aye to aye!

Why couldn't the pirate play cards? Because he was sitting on the deck.

What's a pirate's favorite exercise? The plank.

Why did the pirate buy an eyepatch? Because he couldn't afford an iPad.

Why do pirates always carry a bar of soap? In case they have to wash up on shore.

How much did the pirate pay for his piercings? A buccaneer.

Why do pirates make terrible comedians? Because their jokes are always arrr-rated.

What did the ocean say to the pirate? Nothing, it just waved.

Why did the pirate go to the party? To have a swashbuckling good time.

What's a pirate's favorite movie? Anything rated arrr!

Why did the pirate go on vacation? To get some arrr and arrr.

What do you call a pirate who steals from the rich and gives to the poor? Robin Hook.

Why did the pirate take a nap? He wanted to catch some Z's.

What's a pirate's favorite instrument? The guitarrr.

Why did the pirate get a job at the bakery? To improve his dough.

What did the pirate say when he turned 80? Aye matey.

Why do pirates like to go fishing? Because they get hooked on it.

Why don't pirates use cell phones? They prefer to talk on a buccaneer.

How do pirates prefer to cook their food? On a barrrbecue.

Why did the pirate get kicked out of school? For arrr-guing with the teacher.

What's a pirate's favorite animal? An arrrdvark.

Why did the pirate break up with his girlfriend? She was too clingy.

Plane Jokes

Why did the scarecrow become a pilot? He was outstanding in his field.

Why don't airplanes play hide and seek? They always get found.

How do you organize a plane trip? You plan-et.

What kind of plane does a vampire fly? A blood vessel.

Why did the plane go to school? To improve its altitude.

Why don't some planes ever get tired? Because they always stay on course.

What do you call a plane that tells jokes? A high-flyer.

Why was the plane always calm? It knew how to stay grounded.

What's a plane's favorite type of music? Air guitars.

Why did the plane bring a ladder to the airport? To reach the high skies.

How do you make a plane laugh? Tell it a high-flying joke.

Why did the plane stay at the spa? To get a little extra lift.

What do you call a lazy plane? A jet-setter.

Why don't some planes play sports? They're afraid of the crash.

How do you keep a plane from getting lost? Use a flight plan.

What's a plane's favorite game? Sky-high.

Why did the plane go to therapy? It had too many issues.

What's a plane's favorite book? The Sky's the Limit.

Why was the plane so confident? It knew it was always on top of things.

How do you make a plane dance? Put a little boogie in it.

Why did the plane bring a map to the flight? To find its way.

What do you call a plane with no wings? Grounded.

Why did the plane go to the doctor? It wasn't feeling too well.

What's a plane's favorite movie? Top Gun.

Why did the plane go on a diet? To stay light.

Podcast Jokes

Why did the scarecrow start a podcast? He was outstanding in his field.

Why don't some podcasters get lost? They always follow the script.

How do you organize a podcast? You plan-et.

Why don't some podcasts ever get boring? They always have topics.

What do you call a podcast that tells jokes? A pun-cast.

Why was the podcaster always calm? They knew how to stay on air.

What's a podcaster's favorite type of music? Broadcast tunes.

Why did the podcaster bring a ladder to the studio? To reach new heights.

How do you make a podcaster laugh? Tell them a broadcast joke.

Why did the podcaster stay at the spa? To get a little extra relaxation.

What do you call a lazy podcaster? A slack-caster.

Why don't some podcasts ever get tiring? They always have listeners.

How do you keep a podcaster from getting lost? Use a show map.

What's a podcaster's favorite game? 20 Questions.

Why did the podcaster go to therapy? They had too many unresolved issues.

What's a podcaster's favorite book? The Podcast Handbook.

Why was the podcaster so confident? They knew they were always on top.

How do you make a podcaster dance? Put a little boogie in it.

Why did the podcaster bring a map to the studio? To find their way.

What do you call a podcaster with no patience? A slow recorder.

Why did the podcaster go to the doctor? They weren't feeling too broadcast-ready.

What's a podcaster's favorite movie? Pump Up the Volume.

Why did the podcaster go on a diet? To stay fit for the show.

What do you call a podcaster who loves to sing? A broadcast crooner.

Political Jokes

Why did the politician bring a ladder to the speech? To climb the polls.

Why don't some politicians play hide and seek? Good luck hiding from the issues.

What's a politician's favorite type of music? Poll-ka.

Why did the politician bring string to the debate? To tie up loose ends.

Why don't political speeches have commas? Because pauses are too long already.

Why did the politician cross the road? To get to the other spin.

Why was the political campaign so quiet? It had a lot of soundbites.

Why do politicians love camping? It's intense.

Why did the politician go to school? To improve his polling numbers.

What's a politician's favorite game? Follow the leader.

Why was the politician a great dancer? He had two left feet.

Why did the politician go to the gym? To work on his spin.

Why do politicians love smart phones? They love having followers.

Why was the politician always calm? He knew how to stay on message.

Why did the politician get a job at the bakery? He needed more dough.

Why don't politicians play chess? They don't like to put their kings in check.

Why was the politician great at football? He knew how to pass the blame.

Why do politicians love yoga? They're good at stretching the truth.

Why did the politician write a book? He wanted to have a good cover-up.

Why was the politician a great gardener? He knew how to spread the manure.

Why don't politicians trust stairs? They're always up to something.

What's a politician's favorite holiday? Election Day.

Why did the politician go to art school? To learn how to draw support.

Why was the politician a great singer? He knew how to carry a tune.

Why did the politician bring a broom to the office? To sweep things under the rug.

Random Jokes

Why was the tomato blushing? It saw the salad dressing.

Why did the cookie go to the doctor? It felt crumby.

What's a vampire's favorite fruit? A blood orange.

Why did the banana go to the doctor? It wasn't peeling well.

Why did the scarecrow become a neurosurgeon? Because he was outstanding in his field.

Why was the broom late? It swept in.

Reality TV Jokes

Why did the scarecrow join a reality TV show? He was outstanding in his field.

Why don't some reality stars get lost? They always follow the drama.

How do you organize a reality TV show? You plan-et.

Why don't some reality shows ever get boring? They always have drama.

What do you call a reality TV show that tells jokes? A pun-reality.

Why was the reality star always calm? They knew how to stay dramatic.

What's a reality star's favorite type of music? Drama beats.

Why did the reality star bring a ladder to the set? To reach new heights.

How do you make a reality star laugh? Tell them a dramatic joke.

What do you call a lazy reality star? A slack-drama.

Why don't some reality shows ever get tiring? They always have twists.

How do you keep a reality star from getting lost? Use a show map.

What's a reality star's favorite game? Survivor.

Why did the reality star go to therapy? They had too many unresolved issues.

What's a reality star's favorite book? The Reality Show Book.

Why was the reality star so confident? They knew they were always on top.

How do you make a reality star dance? Put a little boogie in it.

Why did the reality star bring a map to the set? To find their way.

What do you call a reality star with no patience? A slow contestant.

Why did the reality star go to the doctor? They weren't feeling too dramatic.

What's a reality star's favorite movie? The Truman Show.

Why did the reality star go on a diet? To stay fit for the show.

What do you call a reality star who loves to sing? A drama crooner.

Relationship Jokes

Why did the scarecrow break up with his girlfriend? He was outstanding in his field and she was just too plain.

Why don't some couples go to the gym? Because some relationships don't work out.

What did one boat say to the other? Are you up for a little row-mance?

Why did the banana go out with the prune? Because it couldn't find a date.

Why was the calendar so popular? Because it had a lot of dates.

What do you call two birds in love? Tweethearts.

Why did the girl bring a ladder to the bar? She heard the drinks were on the house.

Why did the melon jump into the lake? It wanted to be a water-melon.

What do you call a pair of spiders who just got married? Newlywebs.

What did one plate say to the other? Lunch is on me.

Why was the scarecrow so good at his job? He was outstanding in his field.

Retirement Jokes

Why did the scarecrow retire? He was outstanding in his field and needed a break.

Why don't some retirees get lost? They always follow the leisure map.

How do you organize a retirement party? You plan-et.

Why don't some retirees ever get tired? They always have time to relax.

What do you call a retiree that tells jokes? A pun-tired.

Why was the retiree always calm? They knew how to stay relaxed.

What's a retiree's favorite type of music? Easy listening.

Why did the retiree bring a ladder to the party? To reach new heights.

How do you make a retiree laugh? Tell them a leisure joke.

Why did the retiree stay at the spa? To get a little extra relaxation.

What do you call a lazy retiree? A slack-tiree.

Why don't some retirees ever get bored? They always have hobbies.

How do you keep a retiree from getting lost? Use a leisure map.

What's a retiree's favorite game? Bingo.

Why did the retiree go to therapy? They had too many unresolved issues.

What's a retiree's favorite book? The Joy of Not Working.

Why was the retiree so confident? They knew they were always on top of their game.

How do you make a retiree dance? Put a little boogie in it.

Why did the retiree bring a map to the celebration? To find their way.

What do you call a retiree with no patience? A slow relaxer.

Why did the retiree go to the doctor? They weren't feeling too well-rested.

What's a retiree's favorite movie? The Bucket List.

Why did the retiree go on a diet? To stay fit for retirement.

What do you call a retiree who loves to sing? A golden oldie.

Road Trip Jokes

Why did the scarecrow become a road trip planner? He was outstanding in his field.

Why don't some road trippers get lost? They always follow the map.

How do you organize a road trip? You plan-et.

Why don't some road trippers ever get tired? They always have a sense of adventure.

What do you call a road tripper that tells jokes? A pun-derer.

Why was the road tripper always calm? He knew how to stay on course.

What's a driver's favorite type of music? Road trip rock.

Why did the road tripper bring a ladder to the car? To reach new heights.

How do you make a road tripper laugh? Tell them a scenic route joke.

Why did the driver stay at the rest stop? To get a little extra relaxation.

What do you call a lazy road tripper? A slack-packer.

Why don't some road trippers play sports? They're afraid of missing the exit.

How do you keep a driver from getting lost? Use a road map.

What's a road tripper's favorite game? I Spy.

Why did the road tripper go to therapy? He had too many detours.

What's a driver's favorite book? On the Road.

Why was the road trip so confident? It knew it was always a journey.

How do you make a road tripper dance? Put a little boogie in it.

Why did the road tripper bring a map to the highway? To find his way.

What do you call a driver with no patience? A slow speeder.

Why did the road tripper go to the doctor? He wasn't feeling too well-traveled.

What's a road tripper's favorite movie? Planes, Trains & Automobiles.

Why did the driver go on a diet? To stay fit for the trip.

What do you call a road tripper who loves to sing? A car-aoke star.

School Jokes

1. Why did the student bring a ladder to school? To go to high school.

3. What's a snake's favorite subject? Hiss-tory.

4. Why did the teacher wear sunglasses? Because her class was so bright.

5. How do you get straight A's? By using a ruler.

6. What's a pirate's favorite subject? Arrrrt.

7. Why was the music teacher arrested? She got caught with too many notes.

8. Why did the computer go to school? To improve its bytes.

9. Why was the equal sign so humble? Because it wasn't less than or greater than anyone else.

10. Why did the geometry book look so sad? Because it had too many angles.

11. Why don't scientists trust atoms? Because they make up everything!

12. Why did the kid eat his homework? Because his teacher said it was a piece of cake.

14. What do you call a teacher who doesn't fart in public? A private tutor.

15. Why did the math teacher break up with the biology teacher? There was no chemistry.

16. Why did the student eat his test? Because the teacher said it was a piece of cake.

17. What did the student say to the math worksheet? I'm not a therapist; solve your own problems!

18. Why was the geometry book sad? Because it had too many angles.

19. How do you get a tissue to dance? Put a little boogie in it.

20. Why did the student bring scissors to class? To cut the class.

21. What do you call a smart cookie? A wise-cracker.

22. Why was the history book cold? Because it was full of dates.

23. Why did the student bring a flashlight to school? Because he wanted to go to night school.

25. Why was the principal's office so cold? Because it was full of drafts.

Puns

I'm reading a book on anti-gravity. It's impossible to put down!

I'd tell you a chemistry joke, but I know I wouldn't get a reaction.

Did you hear about the guy who invented Lifesavers? He made a mint!

I'm on a seafood diet. I see food and I eat it.

The shovel was a groundbreaking invention.

I'm no good at math, but I know my angles.

The man who survived pepper spray and mustard gas is now a seasoned veteran.

I used to be a baker, but I couldn't make enough dough.

I was struggling to figure out how lightning works, but then it struck me.

I wanted to be a professional skateboarder, but I couldn't find my bearings.

Why did the scarecrow become a successful neurosurgeon? He was outstanding in his field.

The magician's secrets were revealed. It was an abracadabra debacle.

Have you heard about the new restaurant on the moon? Great food, no atmosphere.

I used to be a gardener, but I didn't have the thyme.

The bicycle can't stand on its own because it's two-tired.

A boiled egg in the morning is hard to beat.

I'm a big fan of whiteboards. They're re-markable.

Did you hear about the mathematician who's afraid of negative numbers? He will stop at nothing to avoid them.

I used to be a watchmaker. It was just a matter of time.

The future, the present, and the past walk into a bar. Things got a little tense.

I'm reading a book about anti-gravity. It's impossible to put down.

When the past, present, and future go camping, they always argue. It's intense.

I wondered why the baseball was getting bigger. Then it hit me.

Sci-Fi Jokes

Why don't aliens use computers? They prefer space stations.

Why don't sci-fi characters get lost? They always follow the star map.

How do you organize a sci-fi mission? You plan-et.

Why did the astronaut go to school? To improve his space knowledge.

Why don't some robots ever get tired? They always have energy cells.

What do you call a sci-fi character that tells jokes? A pun-oid.

What's a sci-fi character's favorite type of music? Space jams.

Why did the robot bring a ladder to the spaceship? To reach new heights.

How do you make a sci-fi character laugh? Tell them an out-of-this-world joke.

What do you call a lazy robot? A slack-droid.

How do you keep a sci-fi character from getting lost? Use a galaxy map.

What's a sci-fi character's favorite game? Space tag.

Why did the robot go to therapy? It had too many issues.

What's a sci-fi character's favorite book? Dune.

Why was the sci-fi character so confident? They knew they were always on solid ground.

How do you make a sci-fi character dance? Put a little boogie in it.

Why did the astronaut bring a map to the adventure? To find his way.

What do you call a sci-fi character with no patience? A slow-bot.

What's a sci-fi character's favorite movie? Star Wars.

Why did the sci-fi character go on a diet? To stay in shape.

What do you call a sci-fi character who loves to sing? A space-melody.

Science Jokes

Why can't you trust an atom? Because they make up everything.

Why are chemists excellent for solving problems? They have all the solutions.

What do you call an educated tube? A graduated cylinder.

Why did the biologist look forward to casual Fridays? Because they're gene-therapy days.

Why did the physics teacher break up with the biology teacher? There was no chemistry.

How does a scientist freshen her breath? With experi-mints.

What did the scientist say when he found 2 isotopes of helium? HeHe.

How do you know the moon is going broke? It's down to its last quarter.

What did the stamen say to the pistil? I like your style.

Why do chemists like nitrates so much? They're cheaper than day rates.

What did one volcano say to the other? I lava you.

How does a biologist keep in touch? Cell phone.

Why was the cell phone wearing glasses? It lost its contacts.

Why can't you trust atoms? They make up everything.

Why was the mushroom invited to the party? Because he was a fungi.

Why didn't the skeleton go to the party? He had no body to go with.

Why did the germ cross the microscope? To get to the other slide.

Why did the bear dissolve in water? It was polar.

What did one DNA strand say to the other? Do these genes make my butt look big?

Why did the cloud date the fog? He was so down to earth.

Why are chemists bad at school? They can't find the solutions.

What is a physicist's favorite food? Fission chips.

Senior Jokes

Why don't retirees mind being called seniors? Because the term comes with a discount.

Why do retired people smile so much? Because they can't hear you!

How do you know you're old? People call at 9 p.m. and ask, "Did I wake you?"

Why did the senior sit in the rocking chair with his seatbelt on? Because he was a rock 'n' roller!

Why did the old man fall in the well? Because he couldn't see that well.

Why do seniors wear green? To blend in with the furniture.

How do you know you're getting old? When you and your teeth don't sleep together.

Why did the retiree start gardening? To weed out his worries.

What's the best part about turning 65? Kidnappers are not very interested in you.

Why did the senior join the choir? He wanted to sing the oldies but goodies.

What do seniors eat for breakfast? Oatmeal and memories.

Why do seniors tell bad jokes? Because the old ones are the best!

What did the senior give his wife for her birthday? A list of all the things she can still do.

How do seniors get exercise? By pushing their luck.

Why do retirees count pennies? Because they're the only ones they can count on.

What's the best way to describe retirement? Twice as much husband on half as much pay.

Why do seniors always read the obituaries? To make sure they're not in them.

How do you know you're getting old? You bend down to tie your shoes and wonder what else you can do while you're down there.

Why did the senior sit in the sun with a bowl of prunes? He was hoping for a little movement.

How do seniors write a letter? They make sure it's large print.

Why don't seniors need alarm clocks? Because their bladders wake them up anyway.

What do you call a retired person who's happy on a Monday? Unemployed.

Why don't seniors play hide and seek? Because it's hard to hide with a cane.

How do you know you're getting old? Your back goes out more than you do.

Why do seniors always know where everything is? Because they've had so many years to put it there.

Shopping Jokes

Why did the scarecrow become a great shopper? He was outstanding in his field.

What did one shopping cart say to the other? "I'll follow you anywhere!"

Why did the man put his money in the blender? He wanted to make some liquid assets.

Why don't some people trust stairs? Because they're always up to something, especially at the mall.

What's a shopper's favorite type of music? Sale-mate.

Why did the shopper bring string to the store? To tie up loose ends.

What do you call a snowman with a shopping list? Frost and Found.

Why did the shoe go to the mall? To find its sole mate.

Why did the tomato go shopping? To ketchup on the sales.

How do you organize a shopping spree? You plan-et.

Why did the scarecrow go to the department store? To find a new hat.

Why don't some people bring umbrellas when they go shopping? Because they know the sales are pouring in.

What do you get when you cross a snowman and a shopper? Frostbite from all the cool deals.

Why did the shopper take a ladder to the store? Because the prices were through the roof.

Why did the computer go shopping? It needed a byte to eat.

Why did the duck go to the department store? It wanted to buy a new bill.

Why did the grape stop in the middle of the store? Because it ran out of juice.

Why did the fashion model go to the store? To get her runway shoes.

Why was the shopper good at chess? Because she knew all the right moves.

Why did the man go shopping with a suitcase? He wanted to carry his bargains home.

Why did the fitness trainer go shopping? To get a new fit.

Why did the scarecrow buy a new jacket? He wanted to look sharp.

Why did the man take a pencil to the store? In case he needed to draw some savings.

What's a shopper's favorite part of the computer? The buy-now button.

Why don't some shoppers ever get bored? Because they're always in good company.

Short Jokes

What do you call cheese that isn't yours? Nacho cheese.

What did the grape do when he got stepped on? Nothing but let out a little wine!

Why was the belt arrested? For holding up the pants.

What's brown and sticky? A stick.

Wordplay

I used to be a baker, but I couldn't make enough dough.

The guy who invented Lifesavers made a mint!

Don't trust atoms. They make up everything!

I once got into so much debt that I couldn't even afford my electricity bills, they were the darkest times of my life.

I lost my job at the bank on my very first day. A woman asked me to check her balance, so I pushed her over.

I tried to catch some fog, but I mist.

The guy who fell onto an upholstery machine is now fully recovered.

Sibling Jokes

Why did the scarecrow get along with his siblings? He was outstanding in his field.

Why don't some siblings ever get lost? Because they always stick together.

How do you organize a sibling rivalry? You plan-et.

Why did the sibling go to school? To learn how to be a little brother or sister.

Why don't some siblings ever get tired? Because they're always in each other's business.

What do you call a sibling that tells jokes? A pun-derful brother or sister.

Why were the siblings always calm? They knew how to stay grounded.

What's a sibling's favorite type of music? Brotherly love songs.

Why did the siblings bring a ladder to the treehouse? To reach new heights together.

How do you make a sibling laugh? Tell them a family-friendly joke.

Why did the siblings stay at the spa? To get a little extra relaxation.

What do you call a lazy sibling? A couch potato.

Why don't some siblings play sports? They're afraid of the competition.

How do you keep a sibling from getting lost? Use a family map.

What's a sibling's favorite game? Tug of war.

Why did the siblings go to therapy? They had too many issues.

What's a sibling's favorite book? Charlotte's Web.

Why were the siblings so confident? They knew they were always on solid ground.

How do you make a sibling dance? Put a little boogie in it.

Why did the siblings bring a map to the adventure? To find their way as a family.

What do you call a sibling with no patience? A slow poke.

Why did the siblings go to the doctor? They weren't feeling too well.

What's a sibling's favorite movie? Lilo & Stitch.

Why did the siblings go on a diet? To stay healthy together.

What do you call siblings who love to sing? A harmony.

Social Media Jokes

Why did the scarecrow become a social media influencer? He was outstanding in his field.

Why did the selfie go to school? It wanted to improve its self-esteem.

Why did the social media marketer break up with Twitter? It was too much of a tweet heart.

What do you call fake Instagram followers? Sham-gram.

Why did the Facebook page get a promotion? Because it was really good at networking.

Why don't some social media managers get lost? They always follow the trends.

Why did the hashtag feel lonely? Because it wasn't trending anymore.

Why did the picture go to jail? It was framed.

What's a social media influencer's favorite type of exercise? Posts and shares.

Why did the LinkedIn profile go to therapy? It needed to work on its connections.

Why did the Instagram post go to art school? To get more likes.

Why was the YouTube video always calm? It had a lot of views.

What do you call a cat on social media? An Insta-cat.

Why did the blogger go broke? Because they couldn't find their niche.

Why don't some people write letters anymore? Because they'd rather post updates.

Why did the social media user bring a ladder to the party? To take their selfie to the next level.

Why did the Facebook page bring a towel? In case it got wet from all the streams.

Why did the Twitter bird go to school? To improve its tweet-eracy.

Why did the Instagrammer get a job at the bakery? They wanted to work on their bread game.

What's a social media manager's favorite snack? Byte-sized treats.

Why did the Snapchat ghost go to therapy? It had too many disappearing issues.

Why did the social media account bring a pencil? To sketch out a plan.

What's a social media star's favorite dessert? Anything with a lot of layers.

Why did the Pinterest board go to school? To get more organized.

Why did the influencer stay indoors? They wanted to go viral.

Space Jokes

Why did the scarecrow become an astronaut? He was outstanding in his field.

What's a space rock's favorite music? Rock-et.

Why did the astronaut break up with the moon? It needed space.

Why don't astronauts ever get hungry in space? Because they have launch (lunch) pads.

Why did the star go to school? To get a little brighter.

Why don't some planets like to play hide and seek? Because they can't hide in the Milky Way.

What do you call a funny comet? A cosmic joke.

Why did the astronaut bring a ladder to space? To reach the stars.

What's an alien's favorite sport? Space-ball.

Why did the sun go to school? To improve its degrees.

Why was the astronaut so calm? It had a lot of space to think.

What do you call a space party? A blast.

Why don't some stars ever get tired? Because they have a lot of energy.

Why did the astronaut sit on the computer? Because it wanted to be a star.

What's a space traveler's favorite chocolate? A Mars bar.

Why did the alien go to school? To learn how to be a little more down to Earth.

Why don't some comets get lost? Because they always follow their tails.

What do you call a space dog? An astro-mutt.

Why did the rocket break up with the satellite? It found it too controlling.

How do you keep a space party secret? You planet in advance.

Why did the astronaut take a nap? To catch some rocket zzz's.

Why was the galaxy so confident? It had a lot of space.

What's a planet's favorite game? Space Invaders.

Why don't some astronauts ever play cards? Because they're always in space.

Sports Jokes

Why did the scarecrow become a successful baseball player? He was outstanding in his field.

Why do basketball players love donuts? Because they dunk them.

Why was the math book sad? It had too many problems to solve.

Why are tennis players bad at relationships? Because love means nothing to them.

Why do football players do well in school? Because they know how to pass.

Why did the football coach go to the bank? To get his quarterback.

Why was Cinderella so bad at soccer? She kept running away from the ball.

Why do swimmers have a hard time keeping secrets? Because they're always spilling the beans.

Why don't some fish play piano? Because you can't tuna fish.

What kind of tea do football players drink? Penal-tea.

Why did the baseball player get arrested? He stole second base.

What is a race car driver's favorite meal? Fast food.

Why do soccer players do well in school? They know how to use their heads.

What did the coach say to the broken vending machine? Give me my quarterback!

Why do golfers wear two pairs of pants? In case they get a hole in one.

What do you get when you cross a basketball player with a geographer? A map dunk.

Why did the soccer ball quit the team? It was tired of getting kicked around.

What's a gymnast's favorite music? Hip-hop.

Why do marathon runners go broke? Because they keep running on empty.

Why did the golfer bring extra socks? In case he got a hole in one.

What is a boxer's favorite drink? Punch.

Why did the bowler bring a pencil to the game? To draw a strike.

What do you call a boomerang that doesn't come back? A stick.

Why was the baseball team always at the piano? Because they needed to practice their pitch.

Student Jokes

Why don't some students ever get lost? They always follow the school rules.

Why did the scarecrow get good grades? He was outstanding in his field.

What did one pencil say to the other? "You're looking sharp!"

Why did the student bring a ladder to school? To go to high school.

Why did the music teacher go to jail? Because she got caught with too many notes.

Why did the student take a ruler to bed? To see how long he slept.

What do you call a student who loves math? A number cruncher.

Why don't some students trust stairs? They're always up to something.

Why did the student bring a flashlight to school? Because he wanted to go to night school.

Why was the math book sad? It had too many problems.

Why did the student sit on the clock? He wanted to be on time.

What did the student say to the math worksheet? "I'm not a therapist; solve your own problems!"

Why was the geometry book sad? Because it had too many angles.

Why did the student bring scissors to class? To cut the class.

What do you call a smart cookie? A wise-cracker.

Why was the history book cold? Because it was full of dates.

Why did the student bring a flashlight to school? To go to night school.

Why did the student bring a rope to school? To tie up loose ends.

Why did the student sit in the corner during lunch? Because he wanted a square meal.

Why don't some students eat pencils? Because it's pointless.

Why did the student take a book to the beach? To catch up on his reading.

Why did the student bring a pencil to class? To draw attention.

Why did the scarecrow become a great student? He was outstanding in his field.

Superhero Jokes

Why did the superhero flush the toilet? Because it was his duty.

Why don't superheroes get lost? They always have their capes pointed north.

How do you organize a superhero party? You plan-et.

Why did the superhero go to school? To improve his super-knowledge.

Why don't superheroes ever get tired? They always have super energy.

What do you call a superhero that tells jokes? A pun-isher.

Why was the superhero always calm? He knew how to stay grounded.

What's a superhero's favorite type of music? Heavy metal.

Why did the superhero bring a ladder to the rescue? To reach new heights.

How do you make a superhero laugh? Tell him a super joke.

Why did the superhero stay at the spa? To get a little extra relaxation.

What do you call a lazy superhero? A slack-tivist.

Why don't superheroes play sports? They're afraid of breaking the rules.

How do you keep a superhero from getting lost? Use a hero map.

What's a superhero's favorite game? Capture the villain.

Why did the superhero go to therapy? He had too many issues.

What's a superhero's favorite book? The Amazing Adventures of Kavalier & Clay.

Why was the superhero so confident? He knew he was always on solid ground.

How do you make a superhero dance? Put a little boogie in it.

Why did the superhero bring a map to the adventure? To find his way.

What do you call a superhero with no patience? A slow-poke.

Why did the superhero go to the doctor? He wasn't feeling too well.

What's a superhero's favorite movie? The Incredibles.

Why did the superhero go on a diet? To stay in shape.

What do you call a superhero who loves to sing? A super-melody.

TV Jokes

Why don't TVs play hide and seek? Because they always get caught in the screen.

What's a TV's favorite kind of weather? Channeling sunshine.

Why did the TV go to school? To improve its screenplay.

Why do actors in TV shows never get lost? Because they always have a script.

Why don't TVs make good friends? They're always on the screen.

Why did the TV go to the beach? To improve its reception.

How do you organize a TV show party? You stream it.

Why did the reality show break up with the soap opera? It found it too dramatic.

What do you call a TV show about gardening? Lawn and Order.

Why was the TV so good at sports? Because it had a great receiver.

Why don't TVs go to the gym? They're already in great shape.

What do you get when you cross a TV with a dog? A Golden Retriever (for awards shows).

Why did the sitcom go to therapy? It had too many issues.

Why did the TV producer go to jail? For too much screen time.

What do you call a TV show about cats? Claw and Order.

Why did the news anchor go to jail? For making a scene.

Why did the TV go to the doctor? It had a bad case of the static.

What's a TV's favorite music? Remote control.

Why was the TV show about fishing canceled? It couldn't reel in viewers.

What did the TV say to the remote? "You turn me on!"

Why did the TV chef go to jail? For too much seasoning.

What's a TV's favorite type of book? One with a good plot.

Why was the TV detective so good at solving cases? It always had the best clues.

Why don't TVs play sports? They might break down during a match.

What's a TV's favorite animal? A channel catfish.

Talent Show Jokes

Why did the scarecrow join the talent show? He was outstanding in his field.

Why don't some contestants get lost? They always follow the spotlight.

How do you organize a talent show? You plan-et.

Why did the performer go to school? To improve their stage presence.

Why don't some talent shows ever get boring? They always have talent.

What do you call a talent show that tells jokes? A pun-derful contest.

Why was the talent show host always calm? They knew how to stay in control.

What's a performer's favorite type of music? Talent tunes.

How do you make a talent show contestant laugh? Tell them a showstopper joke.

Why did the contestant stay at the spa? To get a little extra relaxation.

What do you call a lazy contestant? A slack-talent.

Why don't some talent shows ever get boring? They always have applause.

How do you keep a contestant from getting lost? Use a talent map.

What's a talent show's favorite game? Simon says.

Why did the contestant go to therapy? They had too many unresolved issues.

What's a talent show's favorite book? Talent is Overrated.

Why was the contestant so confident? They knew they were always on top.

How do you make a contestant dance? Put a little boogie in it.

Why did the performer bring a map to the show? To find their way.

What do you call a talent show contestant with no patience? A slow star.

Why did the contestant go to the doctor? They weren't feeling too talented.

What's a talent show's favorite movie? America's Got Talent.

Why did the contestant go on a diet? To stay fit for the performance.

What do you call a talent show contestant who loves to sing? A talent crooner.

Teacher Jokes

Why did the scarecrow become a great teacher? He was outstanding in his field.

Why don't some teachers tell secrets in the hallway? Because they have too many ears.

Why did the teacher wear sunglasses? Because her class was so bright.

Why did the math book look sad? It had too many problems.

Why did the teacher bring a ladder to class? To reach the high grades.

Why did the teacher go to jail? For holding too many classes.

How do teachers freshen their breath? With ex-pel-mints.

Why did the teacher bring a fishing net to school? To catch up on her students.

What do you call a teacher who doesn't fart in public? A private tutor.

Why did the teacher sit on the clock? She wanted to be on time.

Why did the geography teacher go to jail? For crossing state lines.

Why don't some teachers get bored in class? Because they always have pupils.

Why was the music teacher arrested? She got caught with too many notes.

Why did the teacher write on the window? Because she wanted the lesson to be clear.

What's a teacher's favorite nation? Expla-nation.

Why did the teacher take a nap during class? Because she wanted to sleep on it.

Why did the teacher go to the beach? To test the water.

Why did the teacher bring a broom to school? To sweep through the lesson.

Why did the teacher become a librarian? Because she liked the novel approach.

Why don't some teachers trust atoms? Because they make up everything!

Why did the teacher bring a radio to class? To tune into her students.

What do you call a teacher who loves math? A problem solver.

Why did the teacher bring a snake to school? To teach hiss-tory.

Why did the teacher go to therapy? She had too many issues with her pupils.

Tech Jokes

2. Why was the smartphone wearing glasses? It lost its contacts.

3. How does a computer get drunk? It takes screenshots.

4. Why was the computer cold? It left its Windows open.

5. Why don't programmers like nature? It has too many bugs.

6. Why do Java developers wear glasses? Because they don't C#.

7. What did the computer do at lunchtime? Had a byte.

8. Why did the PowerPoint presentation cross the road? To get to the other slide.

9. How do you comfort a JavaScript bug? You console it.

10. Why was the robot angry? People kept pushing its buttons.

11. Why did the IT guy go broke? He couldn't find his cache.

12. What do you call a computer superhero? A Screen Saver.

13. How does a computer tell you it needs more memory? It says "Byte me!"

14. Why was the cell phone so relaxed? Because it was in airplane mode.

15. Why don't computers play tennis? Too many nets.

16. How did the hacker escape the police? He just ransomware.

18. Why was the computer always tired? It had too many tasks running.

19. Why did the server go broke? Because it couldn't handle the cache flow.

20. How do you make a motherboard smile? Just "chip" away at it.

21. Why did the Wi-Fi go to school? To improve its signal strength.

22. Why don't computers trust each other? They have too many bytes.

23. Why did the computer squeak? Because someone stepped on its mouse!

24. How do computers get out of the forest? They use the 'Escape' key.

25. Why was the computer a good singer? It had a great hard drive.

Technology Jokes

Why don't some computers ever get tired? They have all the right components.

How does a computer get drunk? It takes screenshots.

Why did the smartphone wear glasses? It lost its contacts.

Why was the computer so smart? It had a lot of bytes.

What's a computer's favorite snack? Microchips.

Why don't some programmers like nature? It has too many bugs.

Why do Java developers wear glasses? Because they don't C#.

Why did the computer break up with the internet? It found it too connected.

What do you call a computer superhero? A screen saver.

How do you comfort a JavaScript bug? You console it.

Why did the robot go on vacation? It needed to recharge.

Why was the robot angry? People kept pushing its buttons.

Why did the IT guy go broke? He couldn't find his cache.

What do you call a computer's sneeze? A-choo.

What did the computer do at lunchtime? Had a byte.

Why was the cell phone so relaxed? Because it was in airplane mode.

Why don't some computers play tennis? They might crash.

Why did the laptop need a break? It was feeling drained.

What do you get when you cross a computer and a lifeguard? A screen saver.

How did the hacker escape the police? He just ransomware.

Why did the computer squeak? Because someone stepped on its mouse!

Theater Jokes

Why don't actors ever get lost? They always follow the script.

How do you organize a play? You plan-et.

Why did the actor go to school? To improve his stage presence.

Why don't some actors ever get tired? They're always in character.

What do you call an actor that tells jokes? A pun-dit.

Why was the director always calm? He knew how to stay grounded.

What's an actor's favorite type of music? Show tunes.

Why did the actor bring a ladder to the stage? To reach new heights.

How do you make an actor laugh? Tell them a theatrical joke.

Why did the actor stay at the spa? To get a little extra relaxation.

What do you call a lazy actor? A slack-tor.

Why don't some actors play sports? They're afraid of missing their cues.

How do you keep an actor from getting lost? Use a theater map.

What's an actor's favorite game? Charades.

Why did the actor go to therapy? He had too many unresolved issues.

What's an actor's favorite book? Hamlet.

Why was the actor so confident? He knew he was always on solid ground.

How do you make an actor dance? Put a little boogie in it.

Why did the actor bring a map to the audition? To find his way.

What do you call an actor with no patience? A slow-thespian.

Why did the actor go to the doctor? He wasn't feeling too well.

What's an actor's favorite movie? Shakespeare in Love.

Why did the actor go on a diet? To stay fit for the role.

What do you call an actor who loves to sing? A mel-actor.

How do you make a playwright cry? Critique their work.

Train Jokes

Why did the scarecrow become a great conductor? He was outstanding in his field.

What kind of train does a teacher ride? The grade train.

Why don't trains play hide and seek? They always get found.

How do you organize a train trip? You plan-et.

Why did the train go to school? To improve its track record.

Why don't some trains ever get tired? Because they always stay on track.

What do you call a train that tells jokes? A loco-motive.

Why was the train always calm? It knew how to stay on the rails.

What's a train's favorite type of music? Heavy metal.

Why did the train bring a ladder to the station? To reach the high speeds.

How do you make a train laugh? Tell it a rail-y good joke.

Why did the train stay at the spa? To get a little extra steam.

What do you call a lazy train? A sleeper.

Why don't some trains play sports? They're afraid of the derail.

How do you keep a train from getting lost? Use a railway map.

What's a train's favorite game? Track and field.

Why did the train go to therapy? It had too many issues.

What's a train's favorite book? The Little Engine That Could.

Why was the train so confident? It knew it was always on the right track.

How do you make a train dance? Put a little boogie in it.

Why did the train bring a map to the journey? To find its way.

What do you call a train with no wheels? A slowpoke.

Why did the train go to the doctor? It wasn't feeling too well.

What's a train's favorite movie? Polar Express.

Why did the train go on a diet? To stay light on the tracks.

Travel Jokes

What do you call a snowman on vacation? A chill tourist.

Why did the scarecrow become a successful traveler? He was outstanding in his field.

What do you call a canary in a suitcase? A stowaway.

Why don't oysters travel on airplanes? Because they're shellfish.

Why did the airplane get sent to its room? It had a bad altitude.

What's a pirate's favorite country to visit? Arrrgentina.

Why did the golfer bring two pairs of pants on vacation? In case he got a hole in one.

How do oceans say goodbye? They wave.

Why did the bicycle go on vacation? It was two-tired.

What do you get when you cross a plane with a magician? A flying sorcerer.

Why did the map go to school? To improve its sense of direction.

What's a cow's favorite place to go on vacation? Moo York City.

Why don't tourists ever get lost? They always know the way to the hotel.

Why did the beach refuse to wave back? It was tide.

Why don't some people travel to the moon? Because they need more space.

How do you organize a space-themed vacation? You planet.

Why did the sand blush? Because the sea weed.

What did the ocean say to the airplane? Nothing, it just waved.

Why did the airplane sit by itself at the airport? It had terminal issues.

What do you call a dog that travels? A rover.

Why did the mountain climber go to art school? To get a better peak.

Why do travelers never get bored? They always have interesting journeys.

What's a snowman's favorite vacation spot? The North Pool.

Why did the hotel guest bring a suitcase to the buffet? Because it was all-you-can-eat.

Vacation Jokes

Why did the scarecrow become a travel agent? He was outstanding in his field.

Why don't some people get lost on vacation? They always follow the itinerary.

How do you organize a vacation? You plan-et.

Why don't some travelers ever get tired? They always have a sense of adventure.

What do you call a tourist that tells jokes? A pun-derer.

Why was the vacationer always calm? He knew how to stay relaxed.

What's a traveler's favorite type of music? Road trip rock.

Why did the tourist bring a ladder to the beach? To reach new heights.

How do you make a tourist laugh? Tell them a destination joke.

Why did the beachgoer stay at the spa? To get a little extra relaxation.

What do you call a lazy vacationer? A slack-packer.

Why don't some tourists play sports? They're afraid of missing their flight.

How do you keep a traveler from getting lost? Use a vacation map.

What's a vacationer's favorite game? Travel bingo.

Why did the traveler go to therapy? He had too many baggage issues.

What's a tourist's favorite book? Eat, Pray, Love.

Why was the vacation so confident? It knew it was always a getaway.

How do you make a tourist dance? Put a little boogie in it.

Why did the vacationer bring a map to the resort? To find his way.

What do you call a traveler with no patience? A slow tripper.

Why did the beachgoer go to the doctor? He wasn't feeling too sandy.

What's a vacationer's favorite movie? National Lampoon's Vacation.

Why did the tourist go on a diet? To stay fit for the trip.

What do you call a traveler who loves to sing? A tour-de-force.

Vegetarian Jokes

Why did the tomato blush? Because it saw the salad dressing.

Why did the cucumber call 911? Because it was in a pickle.

Why do potatoes make good detectives? Because they keep their eyes peeled.

How do you turn a soup into gold? Add 24 carrots.

Why did the corn go to the doctor? Because it had an earache.

What's a vegetarian's favorite martial art? Tofu-fu.

Why don't vegetables ever play hide and seek? Because they always get caught.

Why did the broccoli break up with the mushroom? Because he didn't have much room.

What do you call a lazy pea? A couch potato.

Why was the carrot embarrassed? Because it saw the salad dressing.

Why don't vegetarians fight? They don't want to squash their problems.

What's a vegetarian's favorite game? Boggle.

Why did the tomato turn red? Because it couldn't find a date.

What do you call a vegetarian werewolf? A beet-eater.

Why did the vegetable band break up? Because it couldn't beet the competition.

Why did the tofu cross the road? To prove it wasn't chicken.

How do you make a vegetable laugh? Tell it a corny joke.

Why was the vegetable garden so bad at secrets? Because it was full of leeks.

Why did the lettuce go to the beach? Because it wanted to get some sun.

How do vegetarians discipline their kids? They give them a timeout in the thyme.

Why did the zucchini join the band? Because it wanted to play the squash drums.

What's a vegetarian's favorite sport? Squash.

Why did the vegetarian start a gardening business? Because she had a green thumb.

Waiter Jokes

Why did the scarecrow become a waiter? He was outstanding in his field.

Why don't some waiters get lost? They always follow the menu.

How do you organize a restaurant? You plan-et.

Why don't some waiters ever get tired? They always have a serving of energy.

What do you call a waiter that tells jokes? A pun-derful server.

Why was the waiter always calm? He knew how to stay cool under pressure.

What's a waiter's favorite type of music? Smooth jazz.

Why did the waiter bring a ladder to the restaurant? To reach the top shelf.

How do you make a waiter laugh? Tell them a tip-top joke.

Why did the waiter stay at the spa? To get a little extra relaxation.

What do you call a lazy waiter? A slack-server.

Why don't some waiters play sports? They're afraid of dropping the ball.

How do you keep a waiter from getting lost? Use a restaurant map.

What's a waiter's favorite game? Serve-it.

Why did the waiter go to therapy? He had too many issues to juggle.

What's a waiter's favorite book? Waiting for Godot.

Why was the waiter so confident? He knew he was always on top of things.

How do you make a waiter dance? Put a little boogie in it.

Why did the waiter bring a map to the restaurant? To find his way.

What do you call a waiter with no patience? A slow server.

Why did the waiter go to the doctor? He wasn't feeling too well-served.

What's a waiter's favorite movie? Waiting…

Why did the waiter go on a diet? To stay fit for the restaurant.

What do you call a waiter who loves to sing? A crooner.

Weather Jokes

Why don't some clouds ever get lost? Because they always take the high road.

What's a tornado's favorite game? Twister.

Why did the scarecrow become a meteorologist? He was outstanding in his field.

Why did the man bring a ladder to the weather forecast? Because the temperature was climbing.

What's the weather forecast for Thanksgiving? Fowl weather.

Why don't skeletons fight each other in the rain? They don't have the guts.

Why did the snowman call his dog Frost? Because Frost bites.

How does a hurricane see? With one eye.

Why was the math book sad in the weather forecast? It had too many problems.

Why did the weather reporter go to therapy? To get over his clouded judgment.

How do you organize a rainy day? You cloud it.

Why don't some weather forecasts ever lie? Because they don't want to cause a storm.

What did the tornado say to the sports car? "Want to go for a spin?"

Why did the thunderstorm break up with the sun? It found it too bright.

Why did the scarecrow go inside during the rainstorm? He was feeling a little under the weather.

Why don't some people ever talk about the weather? Because it's always a breeze.

What did one lightning bolt say to the other? "You're shocking!"

Why did the hailstones go to school? To become weather experts.

What's a snowman's favorite drink? Iced tea.

Why did the umbrella go to the party? To weather the storm.

How do you make holy water? You boil the hell out of it.

Why was the sun always so happy? It beams with joy.

What do you call a weather forecaster who breaks the law? A rain-dict.

Why did the wind break up with the weather vane? It couldn't make up its mind.

What's a weather reporter's favorite animal? A rain-deer.

Wine Jokes

What did the grape say when it got stepped on? Nothing, it just let out a little wine.

Why did the wine go to school? To improve its grape.

Why don't wine bottles ever get lost? Because they always find their way to a cork.

Why did the wine break up with the grape? It couldn't handle the pressure.

What's a wine's favorite type of music? Soft rock.

Why was the wine so good at school? Because it had a lot of grape knowledge.

How do you stop a wine from talking? Put a cork in it.

Why did the wine blush? It saw the salad dressing.

What did the grape say to the wine glass? You complete me.

Why don't wine bottles tell secrets? Because they might spill the wine.

Why was the wine bottle always calm? Because it knew how to chill.

What did the wine glass say to the bottle? I'm in it for the long pour.

Why do wine lovers always get invited to parties? Because they bring a lot to the table.

Why did the grape go to the doctor? It wasn't feeling very grape.

Why do wine bottles make terrible DJs? They always skip a beat.

Why did the wine stay at the spa? To get a little extra corking.

How do you make a wine dance? Put a little grape in it.

What's a wine's favorite movie? The Grape Gatsby.

Why did the wine file a police report? It got mugged.

Why was the wine glass always happy? Because it was full of cheer.

How do you know when a wine is lying? Its nose grows.

What's a wine's favorite book? Grapes of Wrath.

Work Jokes

1. Why don't scientists trust atoms? Because they make up everything!

2. Why don't some couples go to the gym? Because some relationships don't work out.

3. Why did the scarecrow get promoted? He was outstanding in his field.

4. Why was the calendar so popular? Because it had a lot of dates.

7. What do you call a fake noodle? An impasta.

13. Why did the bicycle fall over? Because it was two-tired.

15. Why did the worker bring a ladder to work? Because he wanted to go to the next level.

16. What do you call a snowman with a six-pack? An abdominal snowman.

17. Put a little boogie in it.

18. Why don't programmers like nature? Too many bugs.

19. How did the employee's computer get sick? It caught a byte.

20. Why was the belt arrested? For holding up the pants.

21. How do you stay warm in any room? Go to the corner—it's always 90 degrees.

23. What did the paper say to the pencil? Write on!

24. Why was the office so hot? Because all the fans were on vacation.

25. What did one wall say to the other wall? I'll meet you at the corner.

Zookeeper Jokes

Why did the scarecrow become a zookeeper? He was outstanding in his field.

Why don't some animals ever get lost? Because they always stick to the zoo.

How do you organize a zoo event? You plan-et.

Why did the zookeeper go to school? To improve his animal knowledge.

Why don't some zookeepers ever get tired? Because they always stay on their toes.

What do you call a zookeeper that tells jokes? A pun-derful keeper.

Why was the zookeeper always calm? He knew how to stay grounded.

What's a zookeeper's favorite type of music? Zoo-tunes.

Why did the zookeeper bring a ladder to the zoo? To reach new heights.

How do you make a zookeeper laugh? Tell them an animal-friendly joke.

Why did the zookeeper stay at the spa? To get a little extra relaxation.

What do you call a lazy zookeeper? A slack-keeper.

Why don't some zookeepers play sports? They're afraid of the competition.

How do you keep a zookeeper from getting lost? Use a zoo map.

What's a zookeeper's favorite game? Animal tag.

Why did the zookeeper go to therapy? He had too many issues.

What's a zookeeper's favorite book? Charlotte's Web.

Why was the zookeeper so confident? He knew he was always on solid ground.

How do you make a zookeeper dance? Put a little boogie in it.

Why did the zookeeper bring a map to the adventure? To find his way.

What do you call a zookeeper with no patience? A slow keeper.

Why did the zookeeper go to the doctor? He wasn't feeling too well.

What's a zookeeper's favorite movie? Madagascar.

Why did the zookeeper go on a diet? To stay healthy.

What do you call a zookeeper who loves to sing? A harmony.

Manufactured by Amazon.ca
Acheson, AB